CARING
FOR
YOUR CAT

in association with
CATS PROTECTION

D1332461

CARING
FOR
YOUR CAT

in association with
CATS PROTECTION

ANGELA GAIR

ANGELA GAIR

Angela Gair is an experienced writer and editor and has written on many subjects, including painting, gardening and decorating. She is also a life-long cat-lover and is an active member of her local CP Group. She lives in London with her two cats, Charlie and William, who are, of course, CP rescue cats!

First published in hardback in 1997 by
Collins, an imprint of
HarperCollins*Publishers*
77-85 Fulham Palace Road
Hammersmith
London W6 8JB

The Collins website address is:
www.collins.co.uk

Collins is a registered trademark of
HarperCollins Publishers Ltd

This paperback edition first published in 2000

06 05 04 03
9 8 7 6 5 4 3

Angela Gair asserts the moral right to be identified as
the author of this work.

A catalogue record of this book is available from
the British Library

ISBN 0 00 710516 9

This book was created by SP Creative Design for
HarperCollins*Publishers*
Editor: Heather Thomas
Design and production: Rolando Ugolini
Artwork: Rolando Ugolini

Cats Protection is a registered charity
(no. 203644) and HarperCollins is paying 5% of the
recommended retail price of £6.99 to Cats Protection.

Colour reproduction by Colourscan, Singapore
Printed and bound by Printing Express Limited,
Hong Kong

'Simba's helping hand' on page 11 is taken from
The Cat, Nov/Dec 96.

FRONT COVER PHOTOGRAPH: Tony Stone Images
BACK COVER PHOTOGRAPHS: (Clockwise from top left)
David Dalton, David Dalton, Charlie Colmer

Picture credits

DAVID DALTON: pages 3, 8-9, 11, 21, 22, 24, 25 (right),
26, 28, 29 (bottom left), 30, 32, 33, 35, 37 (left), 38-39,
40-41, 41, 42, 43, 44, 47, 48, 49, 50, 51, 54, 55, 57, 58,
59, 61, 62, 68, 69, 70, 71, 72 (bottom), 74, 78, 81, 82-
83, 84, 85, 87, 88, 89, 92 (top), 93, 94, 95, 96, 101, 104,
106, 110
ANGELA GAIR: page 34
CATHY AND GRAHAM GOSLING: pages 46, 97, 111
FIONA MARSH: pages 17, 98
RICHARD PALMER: page 12
ROLANDO UGOLINI: pages 23 (top left), 27 (top left),
27 (top right), 36, 63 (Rambo), 99, 102 (Rambo)
LORNA VERNER: pages 29 (top), 65 (top right), 77
COURTESY OF CATS PROTECTION:
*Many of these photographs were selected from entries
for the annual photographic competition. Cats
Protection is most appreciative of their contribution
to this book.*

Page 6 (Mr D Lowndes), 7 (Italiabella), 9 (Cinderella,
Mrs M E Kelly), 10 (Liquorice, Miss C Hanson), 13
(Thomas, Mrs E V Price), 14 (Sheba, Mrs Johnston,
photograph by James D Farrar), 15 (top left: Mrs J
Slade), 15 (top right: Tinker, Deirdre Mason,
photograph by Vivien Tremayne), 16 (top: Arthur, Mrs
P Morris), 16 (bottom left: Dinki), 16 (bottom right),
17 (right: Rafferty, Jill Waterfield), 18 (Monty, Miss D
Rollins), 19 (top left: Calypso, Mary Caswell), 19
(bottom left: Perchik, Jilly Faulkner), 19 (top right:
Sky, Sheena Groom), 20 (Smokey, Mrs P A Staples), 23
(bottom), 23 (centre right: Big Ted, Sheila Linton), 25
(bottom left), 27 (bottom left: Willow, Mrs
Brassington), 31 (top left: Charlie and Willow the
Tortoise, David Manners), 31 (top right: Jack with
Sabra, Miss S Jones), 37 (top right: Twilight, Cheryl
Hanson), 45 (Cleo and Barney, Debbie Fowler), 53
(Pippin, Mrs B Pybus), 60 (Sir Rupert Williams, Mrs D
Williams), 64 (Sophy, Mrs Janet Boswell), 65 (top left:
Boots, E Baxter), 66 (Twiglet, Kirsty Wigglesworth), 72
(top: Felix, Val Illingworth), 73 (Sapphire, C & J
Scott), 79 (Ecky and Noke, Mrs B A Parsons) 80
(Tipsy, Mr W Harrison), 91 (Poppy, Mrs R Wenzerul),
92 (bottom: Mr D Lowdes), 108, 109 (Katie, Colin
and Jane Weaver), 112 (Casper, Mr D Lowndes)

CONTENTS

FOREWORD

BY THE CATS PROTECTION LEAGUE

'One small cat changes coming home to an empty house, to coming home.' **Lucy Wheeler,** author and poet (from *The Cat Notebook*).

A feline friend is more than 'just a cat' and, for many people, their cats provide them with a love and companionship that is second to none. Responsible cat owners are always keen to find out how to care for their cats and this book will be an invaluable addition to any cat owner's bookshelf.

Unfortunately not every cat is loved, wanted or cared for and The Cats Protection League (CPL) was founded in 1927 by a group of concerned cat owners and breeders appalled by the number of unwanted cats and kittens found on the streets of London. The aims of the League were clearly defined and have remained unchanged since its foundation. They are:

1 To rescue stray and unwanted cats and kittens and to rehabilitate and rehome them where possible.

2 To encourage the neutering of all cats and kittens not required for breeding.

3 To inform the public on the care of cats and kittens.

The League initially had its roots in London, but in the early 1930s it moved to Slough, where it remained until 1977. During these years, about twenty Branches run by unpaid volunteers were established, dedicated to the welfare of cats, and the League's membership grew to around 4,000. An enforced move to Horsham in 1978 saw a dramatic increase in the number of Branches from seventy-six in 1980 to nearly 250 at the end of 1995. At the same time, membership of the League grew from 8,000 to 45,000; a reflection of the League's growing position as the largest charity devoted solely to the welfare of cats and kittens. Every year the League rescues and rehomes in excess of 70,000 cats and kittens and helps to neuter over 90,000. The League also has thirteen large Shelters and expert care is provided at each Shelter by a caring Warden and dedicated staff.

The bulk of the League's work is still carried out by its hard-working volunteers who are frequently referred to as the lifeblood of the charity. Without their commitment, the League would not exist.

The Cats Protection League anticipates continued growth, reflecting the position of cats as the number one domestic pet and the League's prominence as the United Kingdom's principal cat charity.

There are still too many unwanted, ill-treated cats on our streets for the League to consider its work is done.

THE CAT AS A PET

Man's relationship with the cat goes back approximately 4,000 years, although it has not always been a beneficial one for the cat. Things started out well, when cats were worshipped and revered by the Ancient Egyptians. In the East, too, the cat was prized for his ability to control vermin and valued as a protection against evil spirits. With the spread of Christianity in Europe during the Middle Ages, however, things went horribly wrong. For almost 500 years cats were persecuted as agents of the devil. They were considered to be a witch's 'familiar', and both witch and cat were publicly burned to death on feast days.

Fortunately, the seventeenth century was a more prosperous and enlightened age. Cats were accepted and admired once more and their beauty and charm were celebrated in both art and literature.

By Victorian times, cats had become popular pets, and that popularity has increased to such an extent that the cat has now overtaken man's traditional best friend, the dog, as the pet of choice in the United States and Great Britain. The reason for this is

They say people live longer if they live with a cat. What a nice thought for those of us who share our homes with about a dozen of them!

obvious. People today lead busy lives, and many of us aren't able to give a dog all he needs in the way of exercise and attention. Cats, on the other hand, are supremely adaptable creatures and are ideally suited to our modern way of life. They don't need to be taken for long walks and, whereas dogs are likely to suffer if left in the house all day, cats are self-sufficient in this respect, especially if they can nip out through the cat flap into the garden.

True, cats are not obedient like dogs, nor are they as openly adoring of their human companions. They maintain their independence, but they also make affectionate, devoted pets, especially for the elderly and those living on their own. Cats are fairly inexpensive to keep; they are clean and quiet.

They are also graceful, intelligent, amusing and affectionate. I could go on, but I think I may be preaching to a converted audience!

A LEOPARD IN THE LIVING ROOM

The term 'domestic cat' is something of an oxymoron. For while the cat is the perfect embodiment of homely warmth and relaxed contentment, there will always linger the impression that he is just a whisker away from the wild. Even when apparently in a deep sleep, the feline remains constantly alert to the smallest noise or movement. At one instant your pet may be curled up, purring, in a sunny spot in the garden; at the next he is stretched out long and thin like a leopard, slinking silently across the lawn, eyes fixed intently ahead. A tiny rustle in the grass, inaudible to our inferior human ear, has awakened your cat's age-old impulse to hunt. This link

with the wild is one reason why we find the domestic cat so fascinating.

Perhaps, too, we actually admire the cat's untameable independence of spirit; his refusal to be coerced into doing anything he doesn't want to do. Somehow, cats manage to do exactly as they please while getting everything they want. While a dog will happily accept a human as the top dog in his life, the cat answers to no one but himself.

PETS AS THERAPY

Scientific studies have shown that the simple act of stroking a pet lowers the blood pressure, lessens anxiety and promotes a feeling of calm and well-being. The loyalty and affection shown by a dog or cat makes people feel good and touching, stroking and grooming gives pleasure to both owner and pet.

These findings, confirmed by the Royal Society of Medicine in 1991, are being taken seriously and there is now a number of schemes whereby volunteers take dogs and cats into hospitals and hospices to provide

There is strong evidence that cats can be life-enhancing; being in their company is both calming and soothing.

company and affection for people who miss animals in their lives.

SIMBA'S HELPING HAND

When five-year-old Phillip said that he would like a cat of his own, his mother had no idea that a new cat would have such an effect on her other son, three-year-old Adam. Simba duly arrived from the North London Cats Protection League Shelter and made friends with both boys but was particularly friendly with Adam, who is handicapped. Simba's warm, soft fur proved irresistible to Adam. His hands, which had previously been permanently clenched, gradually became unclenched after stroking the cat and are now normal. His mother is delighted with Adam's progress which she attributes to Simba's patience.
Credit: *The Cat*

COLOURFUL CATS

That cute bundle of fur dozing in front of your fire is descended from the African Wild Cat. The tabby markings seen on wild cats provide effective camouflage, the mottled pattern enabling them to merge easily into their background and remain concealed from prey and predators alike. These tabby markings are often seen on domestic cats.

Down the centuries a combination of selective breeding (not to mention unabashed promiscuity on the part of free-ranging cats) has resulted in a riotous melting-pot of coat colours, patterns and markings.

BLACK

A cat that is completely black is comparatively rare. Most black cats (apart from pedigree Black Shorthairs) have a small patch of white fur somewhere on their body, usually under the chin or on the face. The reason for this has to do with medieval superstition. We all know that cats were persecuted during the Middle Ages because they were associated with Devil worship and witchcraft.

Black cats, in particular, were singled out for the worst treatment, but those with a touch of white on their black coats were more likely to be given the benefit of the doubt. A white patch was thought to be a sign of innocence and was referred to as an 'angel's mark'. As a result of this grisly

selection process, totally black cats became exceptionally rare, while those that were black with a touch of white survived.

TABBY

There are several variations on the 'classic' tabby coat pattern. There may be thin dark lines, sometimes breaking into spots or dashes to create a striped 'tiger' effect. There are five types of tabbies: the Mackerel Tabby, the Blotched Tabby, the Spotted Tabby, the Ticked Tabby and the Patched Tabby. The range of colours is enormous and includes black, grey, white, brown, red, cream, silver, fawn and chestnut.

HOW THE TABBY GOT ITS NAME

'Tabby' cats are so called because their mottled coat pattern resembles a type of silk fabric with a watered pattern of the same name. The word 'tabby' is derived from the Al-Attabiya quarter of Baghdad where tabby was originally woven.

TORTOISESHELL

'Torties' have either a mottled and clouded

pattern of black and ginger, or a 'piebald' pattern of ginger, black and white. Tortoiseshell cats are almost invariably female, with the rare male being inevitably sterile. Tortoiseshell and white cats are called 'calico cats' in the United States.

GINGER

For some reason, ginger cats have a reputation for being aggressive. Perhaps it is because of the association between red hair and fiery-tempered females, or perhaps it has something to do with the fact that most ginger cats are male! Whatever the reason, it is undeserved because most gingers are, in fact, placid and loving. Female gingers do occur infrequently and are nearly always sterile. Ginger cats are sometimes referred to as 'marmalade cats'.

BI-COLOURED

This term is often used for any cat with a two-coloured coat but, in fact, it refers to a

RAFFERTY

Four-year-old Rafferty was rescued by a Cats Protection League Branch and then adopted by Jill Waterfield from Uxbridge, Middlesex. Rafferty is very much an outdoor cat and spends most of his days exploring the surrounding undergrowth and riverbank. He returns home with clues as to where he's been attached to his fur: cobwebs, grass and oil. He is timid with people but not with other cats and greets them daily with a rub of the nose and a quick game, but he always ends up wandering off into the distance on his own. At the end of the day he returns home for some food, then sits on Jill's lap sucking his back paws for comfort until he falls asleep dreaming of his travels.

pattern of solid patches of white with one other colour; for example, white and cream, white and orange, white and blue, or white and black. This coat pattern is very common in pet 'moggies' and feral cats.

WHITE

Most all-white cats are pedigrees, but many pet cats are partially white, usually in irregular patches on the lower body. This form of white-masking can appear in different places. White cats usually have yellow/orange or blue eyes and can even have one of each colour. White cats with blue eyes are usually deaf and an odd-eyed white cat will probably be deaf on the side with the blue eye.

There are many ancient stories and legends about white cats, the most famous of which is attributed to Aesop, who wrote about a white cat that was transformed into a princess in order to marry the man she loved.

CHAPTER ONE

ACQUIRING A CAT

When looking for a cat to share your home, you need to decide whether you have the time and energy to cope with a lively young animal or whether a more settled adult cat would suit your lifestyle better. Whatever your final choice, be it a posh pedigree or a mischievous mog, you can be sure that bringing a feline (or two) into your home will reward you with many years of companionship and enjoyment.

FINDING A CAT

Pedigree cats can be obtained from a recognised breeder, and these can be contacted through cat shows and cat magazines. Most people, however, are happy with an ordinary domestic moggie, and there are numerous sources for these.

ANIMAL SHELTERS

At the risk of sounding biased, if you are thinking of giving a cat or kitten a home, think The Cats Protection League! Or indeed any of the many animal rescue centres dotted around the country. Each year the CPL alone has over 75,000 lost, unwanted or abandoned cats and kittens who are beautiful, loving and in need of a caring home. There are advantages in obtaining a cat from a rescue centre, the best of which is the warm glow of

Despite their popularity as pets, cats appear in animal rescue shelters with woeful regularity.

Before you visit a rescue centre, be warned; you will probably go there looking for a fluffy ginger kitten, only to fall in love with a battered old tabby with one eye, an unknown history – and bags of charm!

satisfaction that you get from offering a new life to a cat who has fallen on hard times. In most cases the cat will have had a veterinary health-check, and will have been neutered, if old enough. The volunteers will be able to provide details of the cat's character, allowing you to adopt one that suits your own personality and lifestyle.

If you decide to adopt a rescue cat, be prepared to have your home visited by a home-checker. It is vital to find the right home for an animal which may already have

BIG TED

Big Ted is a giant of a cat, weighing in at about 7 kg (16 lb). This seven-year-old ginger tom was rescued by the Stockport branch of the CPL, having been threatened with an air rifle and poisoning in the block of flats where he lived. He was brought into care with two female cats who were very dependent on him. The female cats in his new home also seem to gravitate towards him as he is so placid. His main interests are food and sunny spots to sleep, and his only failing is a voice like a foghorn!

been through a lot of trauma, so a member of the rescue society will interview you at your home, and follow up in a few weeks' time to check that the cat has settled in well. If the cat or kitten should not, for any reason, settle in at his new home, he can be returned for rehoming. The work of such groups is often

Modern rescue shelters give many lost souls a safe and warm home until a new one can be found.

entirely voluntary and a donation from you is always appreciated so that they can continue to help other unfortunate animals.

WORD OF MOUTH

Another way to find a cat or a kitten is by answering a local advertisement or hearing about a litter through your friends and neighbours. Your local vet may also know of cats that need good homes. In this way, you will be able to see the kitten in his home environment and check that he has been properly cared for. Nowadays, reputable pet shops do not sell puppies or kittens.

KITTEN OR ADULT?

There is nothing more appealing than a fluffy kitten, with his huge eyes and comical ways. However, you should beware of letting your heart rule your head. There is undoubtedly a lot of pleasure and satisfaction in nurturing a kitten and watching him grow up to be a healthy, loving adult cat – so long as your lifestyle allows it. If all the family is out at work or school full time, it is not really wise to acquire a kitten. Kittens need lots of attention and it is very unfair to leave one alone in the house all day.

MAKING THE COMMITMENT

Owning a pet is a long-term commitment, so please ask yourself the following questions before you make any decisions about taking on a cat or kitten.

■ Do you have the facilities to allow your cat outdoors safely? This may not be possible if you live near a main road and don't have a garden.

■ Do you work long hours or go away often? If so, do you have a friend or neighbour who can look after your cat?

■ Does anyone in your household suffer from asthma? Some people are allergic to cats.(If you cannot live without a cat, it might be worth considering a breed such as the Cornish Rex, which has a short curly coat and no guard hairs to shed into the air).

■ Have you allowed for potential expenses such as food, cat litter, vets' bills (including those for neutering and annual inoculations) and possibly boarding catteries during holidays?

■ If you live in rented accommodation, are you allowed under the terms of the lease to keep pets?

■ If you intend having children in the future, can you be certain that you won't suddenly decide to get rid of the cat?

A playful and inquisitive youngster will get into mischief if he is bored, and you may come home to find the living room in tatters. Young kittens also require four small feeds, regularly spaced, a day.

It is worth you considering adopting two kittens, preferably from the same litter. They will settle in more quickly and provide company for each other when you need to leave the house – and you will have double the fun!

THE JOYS OF OLDER CATS

If the family is out of the house a lot, why not consider taking in an adult rescue cat or two? Older cats are quieter and more sensible than kittens. They know the ground rules of living with people and need less supervision. Instead of getting bored and letting off steam by climbing up the curtains in your absence, they are content to spend their time watching the world go by. If there are boisterous young children in the house a small kitten is more vulnerable to accidental harm, while an older cat knows to keep out of the way.

An older cat will appreciate being pampered and reward you with lots of love and purrs.

Older cats are more settled in their ways and they are more home-orientated, affectionate and placid, making them excellent companions. Most owners find that caring for such cats is a very rewarding experience.

These two little foundlings are about to be given a warm and loving home. They will be companions for each other as they grow up.

GETTING PREPARED

Before you bring your cat home you should make preparations for his arrival and make sure that you have all the necessary equipment.

The most important thing is to arrange to collect your new cat when you can be at home for at least the next two days. The house should be as quiet as possible, so Christmas or any other busy time should be avoided. Place the cat's bed, litter tray and feeding bowls in a quiet, warm room ready for his arrival.

SAFETY FIRST

Kittens and nervous cats will seek out the most obscure places to rest or hide, so ensure that any fireplaces and chimneys are temporarily blocked off before bringing your cat home. You should make sure that all the doors and windows are securely closed, too.

EQUIPMENT

Apart from food, obviously, there are a number of things you need to buy for your cat and have ready before he arrives.

■ BED
Your cat will probably be perfectly happy to sleep in a cardboard box, with a doorway cut in one side and lined with a blanket or old

sweaters for warmth. However, there is a wide range of cat beds which you can purchase, ranging from the traditional circular wicker basket with cushion to a sheepskin 'hammock' that hooks over a radiator, with all manner of bean-bags and cosy 'igloos' in between.

■ CARRYING BASKET

This will be useful throughout your cat's life, so it is worth buying a good-quality one. There are various types available, ranging from the traditional wicker basket to the modern versions which are made of plastic-coated wire (see page 58).

■ LITTER TRAY

Even if your cat is going to be allowed outside eventually, he will need a litter tray during the first few weeks. You can opt for a cheap-and-cheerful plastic tray or the deluxe model

featuring a high clip-on lid with an access hole, which prevents him from kicking litter everywhere and also helps to control any unpleasant smells.

There are various types of litter, ranging from the highly absorbent fullers' earth type to compressed wood pellets. Be prepared to experiment with different types until you find one that meets with your cat's approval; some cats, for example, do not like scented litters.

As the litter is soiled, it forms solid clumps which are easily removed with a scoop, leaving the rest of the litter fresh and ready to use. The litter should be changed completely once a week.

LITTER TRAY TIP

Put a good depth of litter in the bottom of the tray; miserly amounts need replacing more often.

■ FEEDING BOWLS

Your cat will need his own bowls for food and water. A heavy glazed bowl is probably better than a plastic one as it is easy to clean and less likely to be tipped over.

■ GROOMING GEAR

Grooming should be a regular part of your cat's routine from an early age (see page 47). Shorthaired cats need a bristle brush and a fine-toothed metal comb. Longhaired cats need a brush and both fine and wide-toothed combs.

Putting on an elasticated collar. You may need some help at first, especially if the cat is nervous and needs a calming influence.

■ COLLAR

If you wish to put a collar on your cat, make sure it is an elasticated or quick-release collar bearing a tag with your address and phone number on it. This will be invaluable if the cat should get lost or become involved in an accident.

■ TOYS

These are important, especially for kittens (see page 70), but they don't need to be elaborate. A simple piece of string or a ping-pong ball can give hours of fun.

■ SCRATCHING POST

Cats scratch to mark their territory as well as to have a good stretch and trim their claws. Most cats with access to a garden will soon select a favourite tree or post for this

At first, simple toys are the best as these can be easily 'sacrificed'.

purpose, but while he is indoors your cat should be provided with a scratching post, otherwise he might decide to use your best sofa. Pet stores offer a variety of scratching posts, but you can easily construct one from a simple log of non-splintering wood attached to a sturdy base, or from a piece of carpet attached to a post or to a wall. Make sure the post is tall enough to give the cat a full stretch and strong enough so he can really pull on it.

A cat 'play station' incorporating scratching post, dangling toys and raised platforms will encourage your cat to play, exercise and scratch – activities vital to a cat's wellbeing.

■ CAT FLAP

A cat flap fitted to an outside door is a boon to cats and cat owners alike, allowing the cat ready access in and out of the house. Various types are available, some of which can be set to 'in only', 'out only', or locked. Some models are activated by a small magnet hung on the cat's collar, thus solving the problem of stray cats wandering into your home uninvited.

If you don't have a suitable door for a cat flap, it is possible to have one built into a hole in an outside wall.

THE HOMECOMING

Smell is very important to cats, so place a towel or an old sweater inside the carrier in which you collect your new cat. It will give him a chance to 'sniff out' your home in advance. On arrival, take the cat to his room, then watch quietly while he inspects every corner! Once he has grown accustomed to this room you can let him out to inspect the rest of the house.

Young kittens may be nervous and bewildered after leaving their mother and litter mates, so offer them lots of stroking and cuddling if they will accept it. It is only natural for everyone to make a fuss of the new arrival, but don't force your attention on him. Wait for him to approach you and don't reach out to grab or pet him. Slowly hold out your hand so he can sniff it, and dangle a piece of string for him to play with.

At first it is best to continue to serve the food your cat is used to, as strange foods might cause him a tummy upset. Then you can gradually introduce the food you want to serve over a period of three or four days (see pages 36–43 for more detailed information on feeding cats).

Once your cat has settled in he should be taken to the vet for a general health check. He or she will be able to advise you about

Proper planning will help to make your cat's arrival in his new home an easy one.

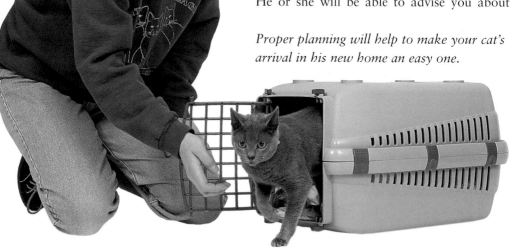

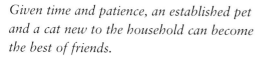

Given time and patience, an established pet and a cat new to the household can become the best of friends.

all aspects of health care: feeding, parasite control, vaccination and neutering. You might also consider having your cat microchipped, in case he should ever get lost (see page 55).

After three weeks or so, when the cat is

FALLING INTO BAD HABITS

You may be tempted to allow your cat to sleep with you for the first night or two, but if you don't intend this to be a permanent arrangement, you must make this clear from the outset. Make up a cosy bed for your cat in a warm room and he will settle down quite happily.

fully familiar with the house, he can be allowed into the garden for short periods (remember that cats should not be allowed out until a week after their initial course of inoculations). Let him out before a meal so he comes back to eat, and always stay with him on the first few occasions.

CATS AND OTHER PETS

If you already have other pets, you should take special care in introducing them to your new cat. To begin with, confine the animals to separate areas of the house to allow the newcomer to get used to his surroundings. When you have been stroking your new cat, transfer his scent to the resident animals by stroking them, and vice versa. This will introduce them to each

HANDLING A CAT

Pick up your cat or kitten by placing one hand under the chest, just behind the front legs. Place the other hand under the rump to support his weight and lift the cat into the crook of your arm. While it is true that a mother cat picks up her kittens by the scruff of the neck, this is only suitable for very young kittens whose bodyweight is light. A cat should never be lifted by the scruff of the neck as it can damage the muscles.

other by smell. After a few days, new and old pets can be gradually introduced under your supervision. Make sure that you keep a firm hold on your dog's collar when he first meets your new cat and never leave them alone together until you are convinced that they are on good terms.

Be careful not to neglect your old pets in favour of the new one as this will make them jealous of the new intruder. In time, most animals sharing a home will rub along together quite happily.

CATS AND BABIES

Introducing a first baby into the household means that life is going to change for everybody, including the resident cat, who has hitherto ruled the roost. At best the cat is likely to be excluded from the proceedings; at worst the parents may be put under pressure to get rid of the cat because of misguided fears that he will smother or scratch the baby and spread disease. In fact, with a little planning and some sensible precautions, babies and cats can live together in perfect harmony. With at least six months before the baby arrives, there is ample time to prepare your cat for the inevitable changes to come. Start by putting the room you intend to use as a nursery out of bounds to the cat, well before your baby is in residence. Very gradually reduce the time you give to the cat to a level you feel you will be able to give after the baby arrives. As you introduce items of baby equipment into the house, let your cat investigate and sniff them.

Caring for the new baby is hard work, but try not to ignore the cat or shoo him away; make a fuss of him so that he does not come to resent this new arrival in his territory. Although a cat would never deliberately harm a baby, it goes without saying that you should not leave a baby and cat alone together; the warmth of the baby and his soft surroundings might prove irresistible to a cat as a place to curl up and sleep. Provide yourself with nets for the cot and pram and make sure they are always stretched taut. Be careful about hygiene. Keep the cat's litter tray and bowl out of reach of toddlers and crawling babies. Similarly, keep the baby's dishes out of the way of an inquisitive cat.

Cats are willing to join in any activity that their favourite human is doing.

CATS AND CHILDREN

Having a pet is an enriching experience for a child, helping to develop the ability to form relationships based on respect, kindness, love and understanding. Children can sometimes be a little too enthusiastic in their displays of affection, however, and should be taught that cats and kittens are not furry toys to be chewed, squeezed and pulled about. Point out that cats are easily frightened by sudden noises or movements, and that tails, ears and whiskers are not for pulling. This is in the interests of the child as well as the cat, as even the most loving cat will scratch and bite if frightened. It is important, too, to teach children not to touch a cat that is sleeping or eating, and to wash their hands after playing with the cat and before eating.

CHAPTER TWO

LOOKING AFTER YOUR CAT

Cats are naturally independent creatures and
will make few demands on you as an owner.
If you take the trouble to provide your cat with
a properly balanced diet, a settled routine and
plenty of love and attention, you will be rewarded
with a contented, loyal and affectionate
companion for many years.

FEEDING

Cats are described as 'obligate carnivores', which means they require high-grade proteins, as well as fats and vital trace elements, that can only be found in animal tissues. For example, cats require an amino acid called taurine, which is vital for healthy eyesight; a deficiency can lead to blindness. Only protein of animal origin contains sufficient taurine to meet the cat's needs. Cats cannot survive on a vegetarian diet!

Variety is the golden rule when catering for your cat; by feeding him a combination of some of the different types of food available –

both fresh and formulated – you will ensure an interesting and balanced diet and prevent him becoming a 'faddy feeder'.

CANNED FOOD

This is probably the most popular food for cats, and there are so many varieties available that even the fussiest feline will be spoilt for choice. On the whole, you get what you pay

Try to provide your cat with a quiet feeding area where he can eat undisturbed.

for; cheaper brands may be bulked out with cereal, whereas the more expensive brands generally contain better-quality protein. Dog food should not be fed to cats. A good-quality canned food formulated for cats will provide all the nutrients (protein, amino-acids, vitamins and minerals) that your cat requires.

DRIED DIETS

These diets are available from good pet shops and veterinary surgeons. They are complete meals, specifically formulated to provide all the required nutrients, including taurine, in the correct amounts. There are different formulations depending on the age and health of your cat. Initially these diets appear expensive, but weight for weight they are

You will need separate bowls for food and water, and each cat should have his own set. Some cats dislike eating from plastic bowls, and most cats prefer a bowl wide enough to accommodate their whiskers!

more economical than canned foods. They are also less messy, less smelly, and they can be left down for the cat throughout the day without the risk of spoilage. The little nuggets may look boring to us, but most cats seem to love them, and their crunchy texture may help to keep their teeth healthy. To avoid overfeeding, the amount recommended on the packet should be weighed out accurately.

Dried diets have in the past been implicated in the cause of urinary problems in male cats. The problem was traced to the high magnesium levels in dry foods, and to the fact that they produced an alkaline urine (a cat's urine should be acid). These problems have now been corrected and good-quality complete dried foods (as opposed to complementary foods) are generally considered safe. However, fresh water must be freely available, and if you think your cat is not drinking enough it may be wise to alternate dried food with canned food. If your cat has urinary problems, consult your vet before feeding dry food.

SEMI-MOIST FOODS

These foods are enjoyed by some cats but they should not be fed exclusively. They come in vacuum-sealed pouches which, once opened, keep fresh for longer than canned food.

DRY BISCUITS

Together with 'treats', these may be sprinkled on your cat's usual food to provide a tasty, crunchy supplement. Dry biscuits are a complementary food only; they should not be fed exclusively as they are low in fat and not particularly nutritious.

FRESH FOOD

The doting owner who feeds his cat only on best steak and smoked salmon is not in fact doing his cat any favours as such a restricted diet is deficient in essential vitamins and minerals. Unless you are a nutritional expert it is safer to rely on a reputable brand of cat food.

FEEDING GUIDELINES

Cats can be fastidious in their eating habits. Here are a few guidelines to help you.

■ Try to feed your cat at regular times each day.

■ Remove any food left over and be sure to wash and rinse the food bowl thoroughly after each meal.

■ Cats prefer to eat food at blood heat (the temperature of freshly killed prey) and not straight from the fridge. This is because they eat by smell as well as taste, and the smell of refridgerated food is 'sealed in' until it is warmed up.

■ Avoid placing food bowls close to the litter tray as cats naturally find this arrangement distasteful.

However, fresh food may be offered a few times each week to provide interest and variety.

Meats, such as cooked beef, lamb and offal, sold for human consumption, are safe for adult cats to eat. Fish, chicken and wild rabbit should be lightly cooked as they can be a source of harmful bacteria and parasites. Wrap the meat in foil and bake or steam it to retain the juices. All minces and offals sold 'for pets only' must also be cooked.

Always remove the bones from poultry and fish as they splinter and sharp fragments could easily become stuck in the cat's throat. Yes, cats kill and eat mice and birds, bones and all, but cooking makes bones indigestible and harder and sharper. Large cooked meat bones, on the other hand, pose no danger. Cats enjoy gnawing them, just as dogs do, and this provides exercise for the jaws and helps keep the teeth and gums healthy by preventing the build-up of tartar.

Most cats love liver, and it is a rich source of vitamin A which helps promote healthy eyesight. However, an excess of vitamin A can cause serious bone disease in cats, so only a small amount of liver should be given, and no more than once a week. Canned sardines, pilchards and tuna are quick and convenient meals, and highly nutritious.

Table scraps are tasty treats for your cat: leftover meat and fat, bacon, fish skin, cheese, yogurt and eggs. Some cats also enjoy a little cooked rice, pasta, potato or vegetables.

SUPPLEMENTS

Cats fed on a well-balanced, varied diet do not need any dietary supplements, except possibly if they have been ill or are nursing kittens. Vitamin and mineral supplements should only be used under veterinary supervision as an excess can be potentially harmful.

WATER

Being of desert origin, cats are very efficient at conserving water. Canned food contains about eighty per cent water, providing the cat with most of its needs. So long as fresh water is always available, don't worry about how little of it your cat seems to be drinking. For cats fed on dry foods, an adequate intake of water is important to prevent urinary problems (see page 103). However, some cats have a peculiar attitude to water; they will ignore their own water bowl but happily drink from a puddle, or sneak a tipple from the bedside water-glass. Others seem to prefer drinking from a running tap, or from the toilet bowl! Indulge the little dears in their whims, as water is important to their well-being.

MILK

Contrary to popular belief, cats don't actually need milk once weaned, and not all cats like it. Some of them suffer from diarrhoea if they drink cow's milk. Special lactose-reduced milks are now available, or you could try giving your cat goat's milk. For kittens, once weaned, diluted evaporated milk is the nearest substitute to the mother cat's milk. Even cats who do like milk should have a supply of fresh water available in addition. Milk is not a substitute for water and should be considered a food supplement.

GRASS

Most cats will chew on grass from time to time, often followed by slight vomiting. It is thought that this is their natural way of obtaining

roughage and of getting rid of fur balls. If your cat is housebound he will appreciate some cocksfoot grass which you can grow for him indoors in a pot on a windowsill.

Seeds are available from The Cats Protection League (see page 126) or from pet shops. Soak the seeds before planting and they germinate quickly. It will also discourage your cat from chewing houseplants, many of which can be poisonous.

HOW MUCH, HOW OFTEN?

The dietary needs of the cat will vary according to its age and health. Unlike some of their owners, cats are usually sensible about their weight and tend not to overeat.

■ **KITTENS** Weaning normally starts at around three weeks old, when kittens can be gradually introduced to

solid food while still getting nourishment from their mother. Begin by offering them a little warm milk once a day (use a proprietary brand of cat's milk substitute, or diluted evaporated milk, which are more nutritious than ordinary cow's milk). Let the kittens lick the milk from your finger at first; they will soon progress to lapping. After a few days, start to give a teaspoon of baby cereal or rice mixed with warm milk, twice a day.

At five to six weeks, a little solid food can be given in place of a milk meal. Canned or dried kitten foods are the best option as they are specifically designed to promote strong growth, containing higher levels of protein and calcium than adult foods. To provide

FEEDING TABLE

Cat	Food	Feeds per day
Kittens		
Around 3 weeks old	A little warm milk – use a proprietary cat's milk substitute or diluted evaporated milk	1
3-4 weeks	A teaspoon of baby cereal or rice mixed with warm milk	2
5-6 weeks	Solids can be given – Canned or dried kitten food	4-5
8 weeks	Fully weaned – 2 teaspoons of solid food	4-5
3-5 months	2 tablespoons of solid food and plenty of fresh water	4
6 months	Increase portions of solid foods	2-3
Adult cats		
Around four heaped teaspoons of fresh food ($^3/_4$ to a whole can of food per day)		2-3
Breeding queens		
Last weeks of pregnancy	Around one and a half times her normal intake	Fed on demand
Feeding her young	Around twice her normal intake with plenty of extra fluids available	Fed on demand
Older cats		
In addition to the cat's normal diet, smaller portions of easily digested foods such as fish, rabbit, chicken and cooked egg with a mineral supplement		Fed on demand

variety, these can be alternated with small portions of cooked, minced fish and chicken.

At eight weeks, kittens are fully weaned and happy to eat solid food – and lots of it! Kittens need a high intake of food to support their rapid rate of growth, but their tiny stomachs can only cope with small amounts of food at a time. They therefore require four to five small meals, spaced throughout the day: two teaspoons per meal for young kittens, graduating to two tablespoons at age three to five months. You may find that kittens eat more readily from a plate rather than a bowl. Plenty of fresh drinking water should also be available. At six months the number of meals can be reduced to two or three and the portions increased.

■ ADULT CATS need fewer but larger meals than kittens. As a rough guide, an average-sized adult cat needs around four heaped tablespoons of fresh food, or around three-quarters to a whole can of food per day, divided into two or three meals.

■ BREEDING QUEENS, like kittens, require a high-energy diet and should be fed little and often. Your vet may also advise giving a vitamin and mineral supplement to promote the healthy development of the kittens. During the last weeks of pregnancy, the queen should be eating one-and-a-half times her normal intake, and at least twice as much when she is feeding her young. She may also drink extra fluids to replace what she is losing through producing milk.

■ OLDER CATS will often want to eat smaller and more frequent meals, and should be fed on demand. In addition to the cat's normal diet, small portions of easily digested sources of protein should be fed, such as fish, rabbit, chicken and cooked eggs, together with a mineral supplement if your vet advises it. If your cat has kidney disease associated with old age, your vet may prescribe a low-protein diet. You may also find that your older cat drinks much more water than before.

In the wild, the cat's traditional diet of small rodents and birds provides a perfect balance of protein, fat, vitamins, minerals, water and roughage. Domesticated cats need a wide and varied diet in order to obtain all of these vital nutrients.

VACCINATIONS

Unless he is vaccinated, your cat runs the risk of contracting one of several life-threatening diseases which include:

■ Feline infectious enteritis
■ Infectious respiratory disease (cat 'flu)
■ Feline leukaemia virus (FeLV)

Feline infectious enteritis may cause sudden death or severe diarrhoea and will kill twenty-five to seventy-five per cent of unvaccinated cats. Cat 'flu causes respiratory symptoms and frequently makes the cat feel ill. FeLV is caused by a virus that may result in cancer, anaemia and may suppress the immune system. It is the greatest infectious cause of death in young cats. Further details of these diseases can be found in Chapter 4. Provided the mother is immune, kittens are usually protected for the first few weeks of life by the immunity passed in their mother's first milk. However, this immunity only lasts for a few weeks and vaccination is necessary to give your cat active protection from disease.

VACCINATING KITTENS

A kitten's vaccination course should start at nine to twelve weeks of age. If you acquire an adult cat and are unsure of his medical history, ask your vet for advice on vaccination straight away. If you already have cats, keep the newcomer separated from the others until he has been vaccinated, and for seven days afterwards.

A course of two vaccinations one month apart is usually given; it is important to keep the cat or kitten indoors until the course is complete, and for a week afterwards, as the immunization effect is not immediate. Booster injections will then be required at yearly intervals, and most vets will give your cat a thorough health check at the same time. After the initial vaccination course your vet will give you a vaccination record card. Keep it in a safe place and take it to the surgery when your cat has his annual boosters so that it can be updated. Reputable boarding catteries will require sight of this record card before accepting your cat.

NEUTERING

A female cat can, in five years, be responsible for over 20,000 descendants. Therefore it is sensible to have your cat neutered. Known as castration for males and spaying for females, neutering is a simple operation which, ideally, is carried out when the cat is about six months old, just before the onset of the cat's puberty. Be guided by your veterinary surgeon.

SPAYING FEMALES

For a female, spaying involves abdominal surgery, and an overnight stay at the surgery. She must be kept indoors until after the

THE FACTS AND FABLES ABOUT NEUTERING

■ Neutered cats are healthier, more affectionate and more contented than un-neutered cats, and they usually live longer.

■ Unneutered toms are more likely to be the victims of road traffic accidents.

■ A female cat can have up to three litters each year and up to five or six in each litter. That can add up to eighteen kittens a year, all requiring good homes. Kittens are cute, but could you find loving homes for them all?

■ Every year The Cats Protection League has the problem of finding new homes for over 75,000 unwanted cats and kittens.

■ It is not 'cruel' to neuter a cat. In fact it is kinder because a domestic cat can really suffer both physically and mentally from the effects of its biological urges. Castration does not force a cat to behave differently, it simply removes the desire to do so; unlike humans, cats cannot perceive themselves as missing out on something!

■ It is an old-wives' tale that a cat will no longer catch mice after being neutered. In fact, the opposite applies as, freed from their hormonal urges, both male and female cats have more time and energy for the sport of hunting. A cat will either be a hunter or not; neutering will not alter this inclination.

■ Cats that are neutered do not get fat. Only overfeeding by the owner makes a cat overweight.

stitches are removed, usually about a week or so after spaying.

Entire female cats (queens) begin 'calling' (come into season) at around five months old. Unless neutered, they will continue to do so about once every three weeks. A calling queen sounds like a baby crying constantly, only louder. A queen that is prevented from mating by being kept indoors will call repeatedly until she (and you!) are irritable and exhausted. And then there is the smell and noise of her intended suitors laying siege to the house. More importantly, for her the frustration of unfulfilled seasons or, conversely, the debilitating effort of constant kittening can actually result in illness. There is a common misconception that a female cat should be allowed to have one litter of kittens before being spayed. As a cat has no anticipation of motherhood, there is no benefit to the cat from having a litter. A female cat is best spayed before she has her first season, when the womb is small and easy to remove.

CASTRATING MALES

Similarly, there are good reasons for having your male cat castrated. It will help prevent him 'spraying' (marking his territory with a very pungent urine) and will also curb his desire to roam far and wide in search of love. This makes tom cats particularly vulnerable to road accidents and fights with rival males. Bite abscesses are a common hazard, along with the attendant risk of infection with serious diseases such as feline immunodeficiency virus (FIV) and feline leukaemia virus (FeLV) which are transmitted through the cats' saliva.

By neutering your cat you are being a responsible owner and helping to lessen the tragedy of unwanted animals. To underline the importance of neutering, The Cats Protection League runs a scheme to help those in financial need to have their cats neutered. Vouchers are available from CPL Headquarters and from local Branches (see useful addresses, page 127).

GROOMING

All self-respecting cats spend a large part of their day washing and grooming in order to keep their coats in pristine condition. Nevertheless, most felines will benefit from being groomed by their owners, too. A regular brush-and-comb session has several benefits:

■ Daily grooming will keep your cat's coat glossy and free of matted hair and tangles as well as stimulating the circulation.

■ A cat keeps his coat clean by continually licking it. Inevitably he will swallow some of the loose hairs, and this can lead to a build-up of fur balls in the stomach (see page 100). Regular combing helps prevent this by removing loose hairs.

■ Daily grooming gives you the opportunity to check for any parasites, such as fleas, ticks and ear mites, as well as making sure that your cat's skin, eyes and teeth are healthy. Black specks in the fur indicate the presence of fleas (see page 86 for information on how to eradicate them). Look for signs of fight wounds, as these can quickly turn septic if left untreated.

■ Another reason for grooming is the sheer pleasure it gives your cat. Cats in social groups will often groom each other, and lone cats will miss out on this. Grooming helps to strengthen the bond between you and your cat.

CARE OF THE CLAWS

Cats normally keep their claws trimmed by scratching and climbing outdoors, or with the use of a scratching post indoors. If they do become overgrown it is best to have them clipped by a veterinary surgeon, who will use a special pair of clippers. Inspection of the claws can be part of your cat's annual check-up. Only the tips of the claws should be cut; the pinkish-coloured quick contains the blood supply and the nerves and, if cut, would cause pain and bleeding.

A scratching post will give your cat hours of pleasure and discourage him from damaging your best sofa with his sharp claws.

DE-CLAWING

De-clawing is a deplorable practice that is prohibited in the UK but is widely practised in the United States, where more cats are kept permanently indoors and therefore more likely to scratch furniture. De-clawing is not the simple clipping of the claws; it is painful amputation involving the full surgical removal of the last joint from each of the cat's toes. It is mutilation, removing the cat's primary means of defence. Please do not even consider it. The humane alternative is to have the cat's claws trimmed regularly so that the sharp ends are removed, and to provide him with a scratching post. If your furniture is more important to you than your cat, don't get a cat in the first place.

Introduce your cat to regular grooming sessions from an early age. Begin by gently stroking him before you start brushing, and talk to him reassuringly if he seems nervous.

Cats are the cleanest animals known to man; they spend up to a third of their waking hours grooming themselves.

GROOMING EQUIPMENT

A selection of grooming implements for longhaired and shorthaired cats. Not all of these are essential; for shorthaired cats all you really need is a flea comb. Clockwise, from top left: rubber brush; bristle brush; slicker brush; blunt-ended scissors for cutting out knots and tangles; fine-toothed metal combs or flea combs; wide-toothed metal comb.

GROOMING A SHORTHAIRED CAT

GROOMING EQUIPMENT

You will need a soft bristle brush and/or a rubber brush, a fine-toothed metal comb and a chamois leather cloth or a piece of silk or velvet.

For most shorthaired cats, one or two sessions a week should be sufficient to help remove loose hairs and keep their coats glossy and smooth. A polish with a chamois leather will bring out the natural gleam of dark-coloured fur.

2 Turn the cat over or hold him under his front legs to raise him upright on his hind legs and gently comb the fur on the underside and chest.

3 Smooth the cat's fur with a bristle brush, working along the lie of the coat.

1 Draw a fine-toothed metal comb from the head towards the tail. Comb the coat gently, first the 'wrong way' to ensure that the deep-lying dead fur is removed. Then comb thoroughly along the lie of the coat.

4 For a really superb finish, use a chamois leather or a piece of silk or velvet to impart a rich, glossy sheen to the cat's fur.

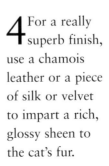

GROOMING A LONGHAIRED CAT

GROOMING EQUIPMENT

You will need a stiff-bristle brush, a wide-toothed comb, and possibly a pair of small, blunt-ended scissors.

Longhaired cats need to be groomed for at least 15 minutes each day if their coats are to remain tangle-free. This applies to non-pedigree cats as well as their more aristocratic relations. A matted coat is painful and if neglected the only remedy might well be to have the matted hair removed under anaesthetic by a vet.

1 Use a wide-toothed comb to gently comb the fur the 'wrong way', one section at a time. Be sure to comb right through to the undercoat to free any knots and tangles. Be gentle on the cat's underparts – a delicate area.

2 To remove tangles, powder them with unperfumed talcum powder, then gently tease them apart with the fingers.

3 Severely knotted clumps may need to be clipped off using a pair of curved scissors. To avoid nicking the cat's skin, always place your thumb and forefinger between the blades and the cat. When most of the knot has been cut away, the rest can then be teased apart with a wide-toothed comb.

4 Brush the coat well, using a bristle brush.

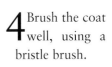

KEEPING YOUR CAT SAFE

Cats are highly inquisitive animals who love to explore and delight in new experiences, although when things go wrong, they may wind up experiencing the delights of the vets' surgery! The old adage that 'curiosity killed the cat' is only too true, but accidents can be prevented by adopting a few sensible precautions, just as one would with young children.

DANGER ZONES OUTDOORS

Even if your cat has access to the outdoors, he is safer kept indoors after dark as this is when he is most at risk from fights with the local strays and from being run over, lost or stolen. At the very least he should have access to the house via a cat flap; it is cruel to shut a cat out at night, especially in winter.

■ TRAFFIC It's odd how some cats can spot a mouse at fifty paces in the black of night, yet they have a completely blind spot when it comes to cars and lorries. If you live near a busy road or a railway you might consider erecting a high fence around your garden, preferably with the top sloping inwards. It can be the ideal compromise; the cat has access to the natural world of the back garden but is prevented from getting near the road. Check with your local planning authority for any height restrictions.

■ CARS Even parked cars can be a danger; always check under your car before starting it up as cats may use them for warmth and shelter. Antifreeze is very toxic and cats can ingest it through licking their paws. Be vigilant and clean up! Cats can also get into cars through open windows and sun roofs and eventually find themselves far from home.

■ OUTBUILDINGS Always check your garden shed and garage before locking them up for the day or going on holiday. A cat can sneak in silently behind you and be accidentally shut in, remaining undiscovered for some time.

■ GARDEN CHEMICALS Many are potentially lethal, so keep your cat away from areas of the garden that have been sprayed or painted with any form of pesticide, weedkiller, lawn fertilizer or wood preservative. Slug pellets containing metaldehyde are poisonous if eaten; instead, try using a 'slug pub' (a small container sunk in the ground and filled with beer; slugs and snails are attracted to it and are trapped). Pet-friendly slug deterrents are available from larger garden centres.

■ GARDEN PONDS, SWIMMING POOLS AND WATER-BUTTS are potentially dangerous, especially to kittens, so cover them with a cat-proof material such as chicken wire.

DANGER ZONES INDOORS

Cats love the cosy warmth of home, but even here there are potential hazards, especially for a kitten or a new arrival.

■ KITCHEN APPLIANCES Cats have been known to clamber into washing machines,

tumble driers, microwaves and ovens and then have come to grief when the owner has unknowingly shut them in and switched on the appliance, so check before closing the door to make sure your cat isn't inside.

■ **POISONOUS PLANTS** Housebound cats may chew pot plants out of boredom, and many, especially ivy, philodendron and poinsettia, are toxic. To prevent this, provide your cat with a pot of fresh greenery such as cocksfoot grass or catmint. To be safe, it is best to view all indoor plants as poisonous.

■ **ELECTRIC CABLES** These may be chewed by mischievous cats and kittens, with fatal consequences if they connect to the wires inside.

■ **HOUSEHOLD CHEMICALS** Make sure that cupboards containing detergents, disinfectants,

medicines and DIY products are inaccessible to your cat. Take special precautions when redecorating; most modern paints, glues etc. contain fungicides that can be lethal to cats if ingested. Keep your cat out of the room until all fumes have dissipated. Never give your cat medicine intended for human consumption.

■ **OPEN FIRES** These should always be protected by a guard, even when unlit. If a cat climbs up the chimney, he will surely come to grief when the fire is lit.

■ **BALCONIES AND WINDOWS** If you live in an upper floor flat, safeguard your cat from falling by placing trellis or wire mesh around the area (it can be concealed with climbing plants).

IDENTIFICATION

It is very important to make sure that your cat or kitten always has some form of identification, either worn on a quick-release safety collar or by a microchip implant, so that he can be identified and returned to you if lost.

When fitting a collar make sure that it isn't too tight. You should be able to slip two fingers comfortably beneath the collar without having to stretch it.

■ COLLARS A collar shows that your cat is not a stray, and with an identification tag bearing your telephone number will enable you to be contacted if he is discovered lost or injured. Never put the cat's name on the collar as this might encourage a would-be thief to entice a trusting feline away.

Some people worry that the collar will catch on something and prevent the cat from struggling free, but this should not happen

MISSING CATS

If your cat goes missing, don't panic immediately. Start with a thorough search of the house; Tiddles may simply have got himself shut in the sock drawer, or decided that the perfect place for a snooze is inside the linings of the curtains. Then call for him outside, tapping the food dish, and listen carefully for any response. If there is no response, ask your neighbours to help by searching their homes and outbuildings. It is also worth enquiring whether any tradesmen's or removal vans have been parked in the immediate vicinity since the cat was last seen; we've all heard tales of 'stowaway' cats ending up many miles from home. If all of this proves fruitless, contact the veterinary surgeons and animal welfare organisations in your area and the local cleansing department to find out if your pet has been picked up.

Place an advertisement in the 'Lost and Found' section of the local paper and post notices on notice-boards, using photos if possible, perhaps offering a reward. Ask the postman, milkman and newspaper delivery boy to keep a look out.

Above all, do not give up hope. Cats have a great ability to survive and some have been known to reappear after weeks and even months. When your cat returns, remember to inform any authorities who have been asked to look for him and take down any notices you have posted.

HOLIDAYS

Never leave your cat to fend for himself when you go away on holiday, even if it is just for a few days. A cat needs warmth, shelter and fresh food and water every day, not to mention love and attention! The best arrangement is to ask a responsible friend or neighbour to visit once or twice a day to feed your cat and reassure him. Make sure you give clear instructions about how to feed and care for him. If possible, leave a telephone number where you can be contacted, and the vet's details, in case of emergencies.

BOARDING CATTERIES

Your cat will probably be happier if left at home, but if this is not possible a boarding cattery is the answer. It is worthwhile inspecting the cattery in advance to make sure your pet will be safe, well cared for and comfortably housed in a clean, warm, airy, individual pen. If your cat is not used to dogs, choose a boarding establishment for cats only as the barking of dogs will alarm and upset your cat. Remember that no reputable cattery will accept your pet without a valid certificate of vaccination (see page 44).

if the collar is fully elasticated or of a quick-release design.

■ MICROCHIPPING is becoming increasingly popular as a means of identification because it is permanent, tamper-proof and with none of the drawbacks involved with collars.

A tiny microchip containing an ID code unique to your cat is implanted by your vet under the loose skin at the back of his neck. The code is then recorded on a central computer database called PetLog, with complete details of the owner. A national network of microchip scanners is held by rescue organisations, such as The Cats Protection League and the RSPCA, and by most veterinary surgeries. If a lost or stolen pet is found it can be scanned to reveal its ID code, and when your details come up on the computer then you will be contacted immediately. Remember that if you move house, you must ensure that you inform the database of your change of address.

Implanting a microchip ensures a permanent means of identifying your cat.

THE TRAVELLING CAT

Unlike dogs, cats are poor travellers. When transporting a cat by car, even on a short journey, always place him in a secure carrier; a loose cat may suddenly panic and pose a dangerous distraction to the driver. If a long journey is involved, do not feed your cat beforehand since he may be sick if he is a bad traveller.

Do not give a sedative or tranquillizer unless your vet specifically advises it; many cats are more disturbed by the resultant loss of control than by the actual journey. Homeopathic remedies are also available to prevent nausea and soothe distress, and these are completely harmless.

Note: you should never give cats sedatives that are intended for humans.

MOVING HOUSE

Moving house is stressful not only for us humans but also for our felines, who generally dislike any disruption of their normal daily routine. There is always a lot to do in the days prior to the move, but it is important to give your cat plenty of attention and reassurance at this time.

PREPARING YOUR CAT

It may be wise to board nervous individuals in a cattery while the move takes place and bring

ADVICE TO TRAVELLERS

■ Before a long journey, prepare your car by lining the back seat with layers of newspaper covered over with plastic. Line the basket/carrier with a thick layer of newspaper. Carry some spare newspaper and a plastic sack for soiled litter and newspaper.
■ Your cat may need to relieve himself in the litter tray, and to be given food and water, but this must be done carefully with all the car doors and windows shut.
■ Many cats pant with anxiety when travelling and this increases water loss from the body. Make sure water is available to him.
■ If possible, travel at night when the roads are quieter and the temperature is cooler.
■ Never leave a cat locked in a car on a hot day since it may get over-heated, leading to collapse and even death.

them to the new house only when the mayhem is over and you have settled in. Otherwise, try to clear a small room in the house about a week before the move and encourage your cat to eat and sleep there. If he gets used to this safe, quiet retreat he will be less traumatized on removal day.

The night before the move, put your cat in his room with everything he needs and settle him down. Lock the door or put a large warning sign on it so that no one can open the door and allow the cat to escape.

*'Aw, mum, do we have to move? I'll have
to make new friends all over again . . .'*

THE DAY OF THE MOVE

When the removal van has gone, put the cat in
his carrier in the car along with his bed, litter
tray, food and water. It is a good idea to take
along a small bag of used litter to place in his
tray on arrival; the smell of his own soiled
litter will be reassuringly familiar in a strange
and frightening environment. Some cats
urinate from nervousness when travelling, so
line the bottom of the carrier with newspaper
and protect the car seat with plastic.

AT THE NEW HOUSE

On arrival, settle your cat in a small room
once again to prevent him escaping and getting
lost in a strange neighbourhood. If possible,
get someone to sit with him as he is bound to be
upset by the unfamiliar smells of his new home
(some of his favourite toys and
perhaps a sweater that smells of
you will help to comfort
him; and don't forget to
put that sample of used

litter in his tray). It is a good idea to leave the cat in his room for a day or two, until some order is restored to the rest of the house. Then gradually allow him to explore his new territory, making sure that all windows and exterior doors are closed. After two to three weeks, once he appears to feel at home, he can be let out into the garden for short periods, under your watchful eye. If he is let out just before feeding time he will not wander far and will readily respond to your call for dinner. Scattering some of his used litter on the soil near the house will help him find his way home. He will, of course, need to wear an elasticated collar bearing his new address and phone number. If you have previously had your cat microchipped, make sure you inform the central database of your change of address. In a very short time he will have marked out his territory and will be quite independent.

CAT CARRIERS

The ideal cat carrier is strong, fastens securely and is easy to clean. It is also large enough to accommodate an adult cat but sufficiently light to carry easily, has good ventilation and allows the cat to see out so he does not feel trapped.

■ **BASKETS** made of plastic-coated wire fit the bill nicely. They also open at the top, which is more convenient because the cat can be lifted into the basket and the lid closed.

■ **LIGHTWEIGHT PLASTIC CARRIERS** with an end opening give a cat some privacy while allowing him to see out. It can be a bit of a battle, however, to get a recalcitrant cat in and out of the end-opening door.

■ **CARDBOARD CARRIERS** are airless and claustrophobic, and they tend to disintegrate if a cat urinates in them. They are also no match at all for a Houdini cat!

■ **WICKER BASKETS** look pretty, but are best suited to docile cats as the straps on the door can wear and break. They are also more difficult to clean.

THE DREADED MOMENT ...

Most cats run a mile at the merest creak of the cat basket, so you will need your wits about you when moving house or planning a trip to the vet's surgery. Lock the cat flap and close all the doors and windows to prevent escape. Then, feigning nonchalance, pick the cat up and try to distract him so he doesn't catch sight of the carrier. Lift him gently but firmly into the carrier, supporting the hindquarters

with one hand and holding the scruff with the other. With end-opening containers it is easiest to place the container door uppermost and carefully lift the cat in vertically. Keep hold of the scruff while you shut the carrier door. Now you can breathe a sigh of relief!

CHAPTER THREE

CAT BEHAVIOUR

A sage once remarked that 'God made the
cat in order that man might have the pleasure
of caressing the lion'. No matter what restrictions
we impose on our pets, no matter how much
we want to protect them, they are still essentially
cats and will always display a certain amount
of wild cat behaviour.

UNDERSTANDING YOUR CAT

Understanding your cat is a question of appreciating the natural instincts that direct his behaviour. Cats have a very strong hunting instinct, for example, which thousands of years of domestication have not dulled. This is part of what it is to be a cat, and attempting to discourage it is fruitless. Ultimately, the greatest love you can show your cat is to offer him respect and affection and yet still allow him the freedom to be a real cat and to follow those natural instincts.

SCENT MARKING

Aside from direct forms of language (voice and touch), cats also have a complex repertoire of scent communication. Scent marking behaviour includes urine spraying, cheek rubbing and scratching. These are all means by which cats leave their personal 'identification card'. Scent marks enable a cat to communicate over long periods of time, and to continue sending messages in his absence.

SPRAYING

A common way of marking out territory is by spraying urine. Although spraying is more commonly associated with unneutered males, it is in fact practised by the majority of cats, be they male, female, neutered or entire, at

Cats greet their friends using body language, just as we do. Tails held erect in greeting, they will sniff one another and rub cheeks, exchanging scents.

some point in their lives. Whereas normal urination is performed in a squatting position, spraying is performed from a standing posture with the cat facing away from the object which is to be marked. Spraying is usually directed against vertical objects such as trees and fence posts, with a small volume of urine being projected backwards onto the object in a series of short squirts. The cat stands close to the target with his tail raised and quivering and his back slightly arched. Often he will also 'paddle' with his hind paws and have a look of extreme concentration on his face.

The scent is believed to convey information about the cat's age, sex, health status and rank, and the freshness of the urine indicates how long ago the cat was in that particular location. This last function is very important in areas where there is a large feline population, since spray signals can be used to help cats to co-ordinate an effective time-sharing system and avoid each other, thus ensuring that potential conflicts are minimized. A fresh scent indicates that a cat has just passed through the area, warning the receiver that confrontation is possible. An old scent indicates that it is safe to pass through. Thus, far from being an aggressive signal designed to assert one cat's authority over other cats in the neighbourhood, the spray mark is used to aid integration and minimize confrontation.

RUBBING AGAINST OBJECTS

Another marking method is that of rubbing against objects. The cat has glands around the head, body and tail that exude a scent which is perceptible to the cat, but imperceptible to

This cat is using his facial scent glands to leave a 'message' for other cats in the neighbourhood.

humans (making it a much more acceptable form of behaviour than spraying!). Indeed, we are enchanted when a cat rubs against our ankles. While this may be seen as a sign of affection on the cat's part, it is also his way of marking you as part of his family.

SCRATCHING

Cats scratch tree trunks and posts not merely as a way of manicuring their claws but also to leave a clear visible sign of their activity, and to deposit scent secretions from special glands in their paws.

HUNTING PREY

The cat is a perfectly designed hunting machine. His entire body, from his claws and teeth to his digestive system, is tuned to a predatory lifestyle. Cats learn to hunt by observing their mothers, who bring back injured prey for them to learn to handle and kill. The behaviour patterns used in the chase are believed to be innate in all felines but the finer points of successful hunting, such as seizing and killing, need to be learned.

A mother cat who is a proficient hunter teaches her kittens the art of the swift nape bite, designed to kill the victim quickly ready for eating. The offspring of inexperienced hunters, however, do not learn the art of the nape bite and may never progress beyond an instinctive interest in movement. This is why some domestic cats 'play' with their victims

Some domestic cats, just like their larger wild cousins, display coat patterns and colours designed for camouflage. This tabby is almost imperceptible against the dappled light and shade cast by twigs and branches.

The cat's ears are important hunting apparatus. Cats can hear high-pitched sounds inaudible to the human ear. There are twenty muscles in each ear, allowing them to rotate through 180 degrees so they can track and pinpoint the tiniest rustle in the grass.

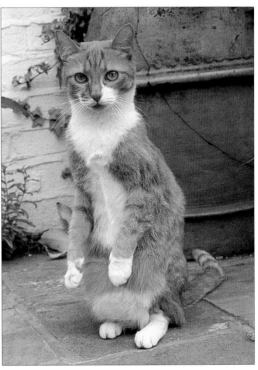

This cat may appear to be sitting up and begging, but the reality is that, essentially, cats are answerable to no one.

instead of despatching them quickly. This is, of course, distressing for us to witness, but it is important to understand that the cat is not being 'cruel'; he is simply an inept hunter.

INTELLIGENCE

Intelligence has often been measured in terms of an animal's willingness to respond to human training, and dogs are claimed to be more intelligent than cats on these grounds. It may not be possible readily to train a cat as you can a dog, but does this failure to respond to our commands necessarily signal a lack of intelligence? It can be argued that an ability to combine independence and co-operation represents not only versatility but also true intelligence. Learning by a combination of observation and association, the cat is constantly aware of his own surroundings and of the actions of those around him. No other animal has undergone such extremes of persecution and worship and yet throughout its long and turbulent history has successfully exploited events and turned them to his advantage.

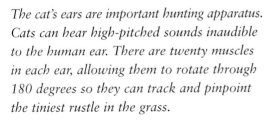

TRAINING YOUR CAT

'Dogs come when they're called; cats take a message and get back to you.' **Mary Bly**

Although cats are generally regarded as untrainable (and most cats do their darndest to perpetuate the theory) it is possible to encourage behaviour that means you and your cat can live together in harmony. Ideally the process should begin while the kitten is young and has not yet developed any bad habits.

Cats, unlike dogs, do not strive to please. Since they are obedient only if this is to their advantage, the best tactics are those of persuasion rather than coercion; for example, by making the scratching post more inviting than the sofa as a manicuring parlour. The most important rule to remember is that rewards are much more effective than punishment.

HOUSE-TRAINING

As cats are very clean animals by nature, house-training is usually straightforward.

1 Place the litter tray in an easily accessible, quiet corner, well away from the feeding area, and make sure your kitten is aware of it. Kittens often need to use the tray after a meal.

2 A very young kitten may need encouragement. Lift him gently on to the tray and stir the litter with a finger to attract his attention.

PRINCIPLES OF TRAINING

■ A cat should never be hit, not even a tiny swat on the rump. Nor should he 'have his nose rubbed in it' if he soils the carpet. Your cat will simply not understand the reason for this harsh treatment and he will react by becoming wary and mistrustful. The stress may even lead him into worse behaviour. Often a firm 'No!' can be sufficient discouragement, especially once your cat learns that obeying your 'No' results in praise and petting.

■ Deterrents to stop unwanted behaviour should come from an indirect source, otherwise your cat may lose his trust in you. Keep out of sight if you are making a loud noise or deliver a sudden squirt from a plant spray or water pistol (to the rump, never the face). Indirect deterrents can be very effective, and the cat won't trace the source of his discomfort back to you.

■ Timing is crucial. Always reward good behaviour immediately with extra affection. Similarly, there is no point in admonishing a cat after the event; you must catch him in the act.

■ Be consistent. If your cat is allowed on the bed or the worktop one day and shooed off it the next, he will become confused and will never learn what is expected of him.

CORRECTING YOUR CAT

Do not punish your kitten if he makes a mistake at first and never rub his nose into it. If you see him about to offend, give a sharp 'No!' and quickly take him to his tray. If a mistake does occur, clean the area thoroughly and remove all traces of the smell to avoid repetition of the soiling.

Give him plenty of praise when he has performed in the tray.

Clean litter is vital because a cat or kitten will not use a dirty tray and may use the carpet instead. Cleaning the litter tray with strong-smelling disinfectants may put your cat off, so use only boiling water and a little mild household detergent and rinse well afterwards. It is important to wear gloves and wash your hands after handling soiled cat litter. Pregnant women should never handle it because of the risk of toxoplasmosis (see page 100).

Once the cat is allowed outside he will probably prefer to use the garden, but the litter

The litter tray on the left has low sides and is suitable for a kitten. Adult cats require a larger box with deeper sides. A plastic scoop is useful for removing soiled litter.

tray should be retained and made available at night, or if the cat is to be shut in the house for any length of time.

USING A CAT FLAP

Fitting a cat flap is an ideal way to give your pet both freedom and security. Most cats quickly learn to use the device, though a few are shy of it at first.

1 Begin training by propping the flap open to show that this is the means of exit and entry. Make sure the flap is firmly fixed so that it cannot drop down to startle the cat.

2 Tempt your cat to step through the hole by placing a tasty titbit on the other side. Then move on to the next stage.

3 Hold the flap half open and coax the cat through as before. When he reaches halfway, very gently lower the flap so that he gets used to the feel of it brushing his back.

4 Next, hold the flap open just a little and help your cat to push it open with his nose. Be sure to give him lots of praise and encouragement.

Don't worry if your cat doesn't seem to get the hang of it straight away; he's probably feigning ignorance. Simply leave him to it and go about your business. Some cats just like to work these things out for themselves, in their own good time.

ROAD SAFETY

Training a cat to stay away from busy roads is not usually necessary since most cats effectively teach themselves to have a healthy respect for traffic. Nevertheless, some cats seem blithely unaware of the dangers of the road and it is a sad fact that many are killed or injured each year.

It may be possible to use 'aversion therapy' to teach your cat that the road outside is a no-go area. The idea is to make staying at home or in the back garden a more attractive proposition than venturing out to the front of the house. All of the cat's pleasant experiences, such as feeding, playing and being fussed over, should be focused in the house and the back garden. This will increase positive associations with these areas and make them places where the cat wants to be. In contrast, the front of the house should be made to seem hostile and uninviting.

Never talk to or pet your cat while he is in the front garden as this might be misconstrued as reward and may serve to make the location seem attractive in the cat's eyes. If you see the cat at the front of the property, either make a loud noise (for example, by dropping a can of stones on the ground) or squirt water at his feet from a water pistol or plant spray. This needs to be done with care, however; the cat must not see you, otherwise he will associate the aversion with you. Also, it is important to make sure that you place yourself between the cat and the road, so as to drive him back to the rear of the property rather than dashing across the road in fright.

When using the water pistol technique, always squirt the water gently and aim for the cat's rump or feet, never his face.

EARLY LEARNING

It is well known that babies can be taught to swim before they can walk, because water holds no fear for them. In the same way, most young kittens are unperturbed by such challenges as being confined in a carrying basket or travelling in a car, things that reduce many an adult cat to a gibbering wreck. Thus, if you have a kitten it is a good idea to get him accustomed to his basket from the outset. While on this training programme, keep the basket permanently in a convenient spot and regularly place a favourite toy or a tasty titbit inside it. You should find that the kitten goes into the basket voluntarily. After a while, try shutting him inside the basket for short periods. Then move on to picking up the basket and walking around the house. Finally, place the basket in the car and take the kitten on a short journey. Early habituation like this will make any future journeys, for example to the vet's surgery, much less stressful affairs for the cat, not to mention his long-suffering owner!

Using the same principle, it is a good idea to accustom your kitten from the outset to letting you groom him and examine his mouth and teeth regularly.

THE PLEASURES OF PLAY

All cats love to play, and their antics provide us with untold pleasure and amusement. Play is essential for the development of kittens because it teaches them important skills that they will need as adults. Kittens engaged in mock combat may look cute, but they are actually learning the serious arts of feline defence and attack. When they dart from behind the sofa and swat a fly, they are practising the hunting routines of stalking, chasing and pouncing. Play and exercise are both important for your pet's well-being, and this applies particularly to indoor cats. If

Cats will continue to play long after kittenhood; they should not be left to their own devices just because they are grown-ups! Just as with people, cats with active minds and bodies remain healthy and alert well into their dotage.

denied the opportunity to express their natural behaviour, they may well become bored and frustrated and, as a result, be more prone to some behavioural problems.

CAT CAPERS

Cats and kittens will happily play with the simplest of things. They're just like children; you buy them an expensive toy and they prefer to play with the box it came in! All felines are fascinated by movement and like nothing better than a piece of string with a feather or a wad of paper tied at the end, either dangled in front of them or dragged along the floor for them to chase. Another favourite is a ping-pong ball or a crumpled ball of tinfoil; these move at the slightest tap of a paw, inciting the cat's innate response to chase and capture them.

Many cats enjoy diving into a large paper bag or ripping it to bits. Another idea is a series of cardboard boxes joined together and linked by popholes. This construction is ideal for kittens in particular, allowing them to rush around inside and play hide-and-seek.

There is a vast array of feline toys on the market, ranging from simple toy mice to elaborate 'cat activity centres'. These are mostly designed to stimulate the cat's natural behaviour, such as stalking, pouncing, batting, chasing, jumping and climbing.Some toys are attached to a length of elastic and can be hung from a doorknob for your cat to chase and bat if you don't have time to play. However, cats and kittens should never be left alone in the house with such toys as it is possible for them to get tangled up in the elastic.

CRAZY FOR CATNIP

The smell of catnip, also known as catmint (*Nepeta cataria*), is curiously attractive to cats. It is believed that they react to an oil (nepetalactone) which is present in the plant and induces a transitory state of well-being in cats. If you have a garden you can provide a lot of pleasure for your cat by growing a patch of catnip for him to roll in. Alternatively, most pet shops sell packets of dried catnip leaves and toys impregnated

Most cats will play happily on their own, but are even more contented if you can find time for at least one daily play session.

the cat rubs against the catnip with cheek and chin before performing shoulder rolls and body rubs, apparently in a state of ecstacy. The effect can last anywhere from ten to thirty minutes.

Kittens do not develop a full response to catnip until about three months of age, and, curiously, some cats never respond to it at all, much to the disappointment of their owners!

Unlike human forms of intoxicant, catnip is not harmful or addictive. Indeed, the response to catnip diminishes with overuse, so for maximum pleasurable effect it is best given sparingly.

with catnip. Just sprinkle some on the floor and watch the good times roll! The sight of a cat intoxicated with catnip is a joy to behold;

THE PROBLEM CAT

'Cats can be very funny, and have the oddest ways of showing they're glad to see you.
Rudimace always peed in our shoes.' **W H Auden**

Cats are generally very adaptable and will take most things in their stride. However, just as with humans, factors such as genetic influence and early life experiences can make some cats more sensitive than others.

There may be a medical cause for sudden changes in a cat's behaviour and the first response should always be to contact your vet and ask for a medical examination. Serious behavioural problems are often the response of a cat to a situation that he simply cannot come to terms with. For example, a cat may begin spray-marking in the house because he feels his territory is being threatened by an intruder, or a cat may persistently scratch the

furniture because he is confined permanently indoors and cannot scratch outside. Once medical causes are ruled out, the behavioural issues need to be investigated.

One very important rule in the approach to treating a cat with a behaviour problem is that punishment is wholly inappropriate. It is upsetting to come home and find that the sofa has been shredded, but retrospective punishment has no effect on the cat's behaviour and merely serves to confuse him. Even if you catch the vandal in the act, punishment is not advised. The cat is behaving perfectly naturally in feline terms and, since stress and anxiety are often causes of the problem in the first place, punishment will only make matters worse.

THE HUMAN TOUCH

Studies have shown that the more mental and physical stimulation kittens experience while they are young, the more friendly and confident they will be as adults. The optimum age for socialization is between two and seven weeks, when they should be gently stroked and handled by a variety of people several times each day (so who needs coaxing to do that?). They should be introduced to a wide range of stimuli, especially to children, adults, dogs and other household pets.

Try looking at things from your cat's point of view and see if you can understand why he behaves in a particular way. This is the key to changing undesirable behaviour into another more acceptable form.

If all your efforts fail, then there are practitioners (pet behaviour counsellors) who specialize in behavioural problems, and your vet may be able to refer you to one of these.

INDOOR SPRAYING

Q *George, our six-year-old male neutered cat, has suddenly started spraying in the house. How can we stop him?*

A First, it is important to recognize that spraying is a form of territory marking and is not the same as urination (please refer to page 62). The problems of inappropriate

indoor marking and indoor toileting are quite distinct and often have separate causes, and thus the approach to treatment is different.

Indoor spraying is one of the most common feline behaviour problems and one of the most difficult for owners to tolerate. All cats can spray urine, whether male or female, neutered or intact, but under normal circumstances such behaviour is confined to marking their outdoor patch (see page 63). Well-adjusted, neutered cats have no need to spray indoors because their home is perceived as being safe and secure. However, if a cat feels threatened or insecure he may feel compelled to mark out his home with his own personal scent.

TREATMENT

All sorts of gambits have been suggested to prevent a cat from spraying indoors, including placing strips of tin foil or pieces of fresh orange peel around favourite spraying sites to deter the offender. However, these are largely ineffectual and can in fact do more harm than good. Cats spray indoors

Cats do not deposit urine near their own food, so try placing bowls of dry cat food around favourite spraying sites (glue the food down if necessary, otherwise the cat will simply eat it and then spray!).

when they perceive a threat to the security of their 'den', and deterrents such as tin foil and orange peel only serve to increase their feelings of anxiety and insecurity and thus exacerbate the problem.

The only long-term solution to the problem of indoor spraying is to take the time to establish the initial cause and deal with that if appropriate. The following possibilities should be considered:

■ Has a new cat, dog, baby or adult been introduced into the household recently? Extra time and attention from you will help to make your cat feel more secure and reduce his feelings of stress. If a new cat or dog has been acquired, it is wrong to assume that the resident cat will automatically welcome him. Try to set aside part of the house where the newcomer is not allowed, until he has come to accept him.

■ Have you recently redecorated or renovated your home? New furniture or carpets or a building extension make the house look and smell strange to a cat. Restricting his access to these areas might help.

■ Has a cat flap been installed recently? Occasionally, the installation of a cat flap blurs the distinction between 'indoors' and 'outdoors' in a cat's mind and he feels compelled to 'anoint' his indoor territory in the same way as he does outdoors. There is also the obvious trauma of a local rival cat entering the cat's inner sanctum via the cat flap. It may be necessary to install a magnetic cat flap, or to board up the cat flap temporarily.

It often helps to decrease the size of the cat's territory in the first stage of treatment in order to increase his level of confidence and aid in increasing his perception of home as a secure den. Temporarily restricting the cat to a particular room in the house or in an indoor pen, along with toys and familiar items, will help to increase his feeling of security. Give him plenty of love and attention, and don't leave him alone for long periods of time.

If all else fails, seek advice from your vet. He may, for example, recommend a recently developed product called a urine-marking inhibitor. This product contains a synthetic version of the feline facial pheromone (deposited by cats when they rub the sides of their heads against objects as a form of scent-marking). Its development resulted from the observations of animal behaviourists, who noted that facial pheromones have a calming function and that cats do not urine mark objects previously marked with facial pheromones. The product is sprayed directly onto the places soiled by the cat as well as on prominent objects that would be attractive places for the cat to mark. It has proved to be very effective in inhibiting urine marking, and has the advantage for the cat that there are no unpleasant side-effects.

Anti-anxiety drugs are sometimes prescribed by veterinary surgeons for this problem but they need to be used in conjunction with behavioural therapy and should not be viewed as a cure in themselves. The urine-marking inhibitor can also be used to help settle cats into new surroundings (and carrying baskets!) because the facial pheromones it contains have a calming effect.

CLEANING

Areas in which a cat sprays should be thoroughly cleaned to prevent 'top-up' spraying as the scent weakens. Never use cleaning products containing ammonia or chlorine as both of these compounds are constituents of cat urine and the cat may perceive them as a rival marker and deliberately respray in response. The best cleaning agent is a warm solution of biological washing powder, which will digest protein in the urine. Rinse and allow to dry, then (assuming we are not talking about antique furniture) wipe or spray with alcohol, such as surgical spirit.

INDOOR TOILETING

Q *Recently my cat Bella has been urinating around the house. I have tried many different repellents but she simply moves to another location. What can I do?*

A The first thing to do is to get your vet to check the cat in case there is some physical problem, such as cystitis or arthritis, that is causing her to soil outside her litter tray. If she is given a clean bill of health the next stage is to identify and deal with the cause of the behaviour. Most often, it is due to problems relating to the litter tray itself, for example:

■ INSUFFICIENT CLEANING Cats are fastidious about personal hygiene and like a clean litter tray. Individual faeces and wet patches should be removed regularly rather than waiting for the whole tray to become dirty. If you have more than one cat, you will need more than one litter tray.

■ UNATTRACTIVE POSITION Is your cat's litter tray sufficiently private? In the wild, cats feel vulnerable when toileting and will always seek out a secluded spot. In the same way, domestic cats prefer to eliminate in a quiet corner and may refuse to use a tray positioned in a busy thoroughfare where they are frequently interrupted. A cat may also refuse to use a litter tray that is placed too close to his feeding dish.

■ TYPE OF LITTER Have you changed the type of litter recently? Some cats dislike litters that release deodorizing scents, and certain compressed wood pellet litters appear to be uncomfortable for cats to stand on.

NOTE: should a mistake occur during house-training, or due to any of the reasons described above, it is vital to clean the spot and remove every trace of the smell, using the method described for indoor sprayers, otherwise the cat may use the same location again.

HUNTING

Q *My cat Charlie is a born hunter and will insist on bringing home his 'trophies' for me to admire. I know that cats are predators, but is there anything I can do to reduce, at least, the level of his hunting?*

A Hunting is a very strong instinct in cats and takes place even when they are well-fed at home. It is a part of their nature so deeply rooted that to try to eliminate it, or even to register your disapproval, will only serve to baffle the cat. The only thing you can do is to take steps to reduce the scale of the carnage and dissuade your cat from bringing

the prey home. For example, you can restrict the cat's opportunities to hunt by keeping him in at times when rodent populations are most active, at dusk and dawn. Make sure the bird table is out of cat reach, or feed birds in the open, where a cat cannot stalk them unnoticed. Some people put a bell on the cat's collar, but ardent hunters can usually figure a way round this one by managing to move so stealthily that the bell doesn't ring anyway! Feeding your cat fresh, gristly meat still attached to the bone might (but only might!) help to satisfy his craving for the kill.

TIMIDITY

Q *I acquired my cat William, aged ten months, from a rescue centre; he had been ill-treated as a young kitten. He gets on well with us, but if visitors come he disappears and will not return until they have gone. He is also terrified of inanimate objects such as shopping bags! How can I help him to come to terms with his fears?*

A Timidity may result from a genetic influence but it also occurs in cats who were not exposed to a range of experiences and handling as a young kitten (see 'Early Learning', page 69). In both cases, the cat learns to take avoiding action in the face of any new challenge, be that in the form of people or shopping bags. Since flight is the primary defence strategy for cats, they do not stick around long enough to find out that the threat is merely imagined. It is pointless to try to draw the cat out of hiding as this will only compound his sense of being under threat. On the other hand,

REASSURING A NERVOUS CAT

Caring for a frightened feline can be challenging, but there is nothing more rewarding than gaining his trust and watching him bloom into a loving and contented companion. Initially you must steel yourself to sit calmly and ignore the cat; any attempt to touch him will be seen as a threat. You must earn his trust before he will be comfortable with your stroking him. Assure him with your tone and with your movements and avoid any eye contact.

To initiate touching, extend your hand towards him very slowly and wait for him to sniff you. Don't attempt to touch him but slowly retract your hand to show that you are not a threat. Offer the cat food to reinforce the positive nature of your interaction. Repeat this process several times over the first few days. After this, the first attempt at stroking should be very gentle, slow and brief. If he backs off, don't chase him. Allow him some time alone before trying again. During this process remember to avoid eye contact and use food to reinforce the positive nature of your interaction.

simply giving up and accepting such behaviour may encourage the cat to become even more reclusive than he was.

The solution involves a process called 'systematic desensitization'. By carefully, gently and gradually exposing the cat to the source of his fear, it is possible to make him see that the terror he imagined does not exist. This can be achieved by placing the cat in an indoor pen along with food, bedding etc. Thus he has a safe haven from which he can view what is going on around him, but from which he cannot escape. In this way he can experience the proximity of children, visitors, other pets (or shopping bags) and come to learn that they are not as threatening as they might appear.

Introduction to the pen is vital so the cat does not see it as a prison. Once he is happy to be in the pen you can begin to use it in treatment. Caution any visitors in advance not to make a fuss of the cat but to ignore him completely. Then gradually increase the cat's exposure to the 'problem', until he learns that its presence is not threatening. When he finally begins to show less anxiety, try opening the door of the pen. With luck, he will eventually emerge from the pen on his own. This process takes a great deal of time, commitment and patience on the part of the owner, but the results can be very rewarding.

SCRATCHING FURNITURE

Q *Spike is a lovely cat but he has a habit of scratching my sofa, which is now in shreds. Why does he do this and how can I stop him?*

A One of the reasons cats scratch is to remove the worn outer sheaths of the claws of their front paws to expose a new sharp claw underneath. Where this is the cat's motivation, scratching furniture is less likely to be a problem if you allow your cat outdoors, where he can strop his claws on the bark of tree trunks.

You can make or buy a scratching post to help direct your cat's attention away from the furniture. The scratching post should be taller than your cat at full stretch (the process of sharpening claws requires the opportunity to stretch right out) and it should have a stable base so that it will not topple.

If your cat has already picked your sofa as his chosen scratching post, place the post close to the sofa. Play with the cat and the post (the post can be made more attractive by rubbing a little catnip on it). Once the cat has begun to use the post, it can then be gradually moved to a more convenient location.

In some cases scratching is also a form of scent marking (cats have special scent glands in their paws), and when this is done inside the house it may well indicate some anxiety or insecurity on the part of the cat. As with indoor spraying (see page 74), the treatment will involve re-establishing the house as a safe haven for the cat.

CHAPTER FOUR

KEEPING YOUR CAT HEALTHY

Cats are generally healthy creatures. They suffer from relatively few diseases and most can either be prevented by vaccination or easily cured with prompt veterinary treatment. The old maxim that 'an ounce of prevention is worth a pound of cure' makes a lot of sense, and you can help ensure a long and healthy life for your cat by feeding a high-quality diet and providing routine vaccinations and regular veterinary check-ups.

THE SIGNS OF ILLNESS

Cats, unlike some humans, tend not to make a fuss when they are unwell. They prefer to retreat to a quiet corner and suffer in silence. For this reason you need to be alert to any changes in your cat's behaviour that might indicate that all is not well. This is where a regular grooming routine proves its value, as close examination of your cat allows you to detect disease conditions at an early stage, when they are most easily treated.

■ THE EARS should be clean and pink inside. Persistent scratching or shaking of the head, and signs of a brown discharge, may indicate the presence of ear mites or infection.

■ THE EYES should be clear and bright. If the 'third eyelid' is visible it may mean that the cat is unwell. Any heavy discharge may be a sign of infection.

■ THE NOSE should be clean and feel slightly moist to the touch. Sneezing and a thick nasal discharge indicate respiratory disease.

■ THE GUMS should be smooth and pink in colour; red, swollen gums indicate gingivitis. Bad breath may be a sign of oral disease or kidney problems.

■ Check the dental health of your cat periodically by lifting the upper lip gently with the thumb. The teeth should be white; if they are coated with brown tartar deposits, arrange for your vet to scale the teeth.

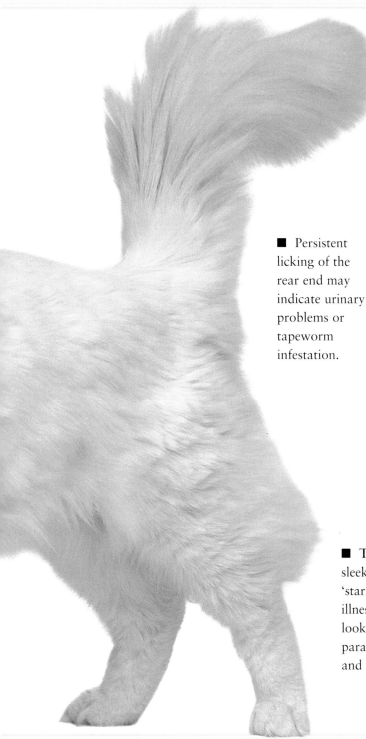

■ Persistent licking of the rear end may indicate urinary problems or tapeworm infestation.

SYMPTOMS OF ILLNESS

The following symptoms should be investigated by your vet. The cause may turn out to be trivial, but if it is something more serious, early diagnosis will give your cat the best chance of a full recovery.

■ Hiding away and not playing or going out
■ Loss of appetite
■ Excessive thirst
■ Sudden weight loss
■ Persistent vomiting
■ Persistent diarrhoea or constipation
■ Frequent or difficult urination
■ Mucus discharge from nose and eyes
■ Coughing or sneezing
■ Abnormal breathing/panting
■ Unusual aggression, especially if touched
■ Staggering or moving oddly

■ THE COAT should be sleek and glossy. A dull, 'staring' coat indicates illness. When grooming, look out for signs of parasites, fight wounds and excessive hair loss.

NURSING A SICK CAT

If your cat is ill or recovering from an operation, good nursing and lots of tender loving care can make all the difference in speeding his recovery. Cats like to hide away when they are not well, so, if possible, set up a 'sick room' in a quiet corner, perhaps with a covered cat bed or a cardboard box lined with blankets, where your cat can feel safe and remain undisturbed.

A sick cat must be kept warm, especially at night. Where any background heating is unavailable, warmth can be provided by an infra-red lamp, a microwaveable pad, a covered hot water bottle or blankets. Sick cats are disinclined to groom themselves, but they can become quite depressed if left in a mess. Gentle combing and brushing will give your cat psychological as well as physical comfort.

FEEDING

Loss of appetite is natural in a sick cat, but don't worry unduly as cats can survive for many days without solid food. However, protein-rich food will certainly aid recovery, so try to tempt the patient with small portions of strong-smelling foods, such as sardines or pilchards, warmed to blood heat. Offer your cat a little Marmite on the end of your finger; this may help to stimulate his appetite. You may need to hand feed him.

Fluids are vitally important, especially where a cat is suffering from vomiting or diarrhoea. You should therefore provide water or a nourishing liquid food, such as beef tea or diluted honey. If the cat refuses to drink, very gently drip the liquid into the side of his mouth using a plastic dropper.

When your cat is ill he will appreciate warmth, peace and quiet, and of course the tender ministrations of his owner.

and liquids – although vets do make it look deceptively easy! Ask whether an alternative liquid preparation is available as you may find this easier to administer to your cat using a plastic dropper.

LIQUIDS

These are best given using a plastic dropper (do not use a glass one). Tilt the head up, insert the tip of the dropper into the space between the canines and the back teeth and slowly squirt the liquid into the mouth. Give only a few drops at a time and allow the cat to swallow after each dose to avoid choking.

ADMINISTERING DRUGS

Be sure to administer all medications exactly as instructed by your vet. For example, note whether tablets are to be given before or after meals and ensure that they are given at evenly spaced intervals throughout the day. It is important, particularly with antibiotics, to complete a full course of tablets and not stop just because the cat seems to be getting better.

Try to give the medication directly rather than disguise it in food, as most cats can detect its odour and will simply eat their way around it or refuse it altogether. Your vet will be able to demonstrate how to administer pills

GIVING YOUR CAT A PILL

1 Place the cat on a raised surface. You may need help from another person, or wrap the cat in a towel. Grasp the head firmly on either side of the jaw. Gently tilt back the head and ease open the mouth by pressing on the corners with your thumb and index finger and pulling the lower jaw down with your middle finger.

2 Push the pill as far back on the tongue as possible. Close the cat's mouth and then stroke his throat until he swallows. Smearing the pill with some butter may sometimes help its passage.

HEALTH PROBLEMS

It is important to be alert to the basic warning signs of feline ill-health, and this section offers a guide to the most common problems affecting cats. Where serious illness is suspected, correct diagnosis and treatment are urgent; consult your vet without delay. All veterinary practices provide a twenty-four-hour service.

SKIN AND COAT PROBLEMS

Most cases of skin disease in cats are due to infestation by parasites, of which fleas are by far the most common. Less common problems arise from abscesses (see page 114), fungal infection, allergic reactions and hormonal imbalance. A dull, 'staring' coat and a disinclination to groom are sure signs that a cat is unwell.

FLEAS

SIGNS AND SYMPTOMS

The presence of fleas is often shown by persistent scratching. Fleas are hard to detect as they move quickly through the cat's fur. You are more likely to find the 'flea dirts', the tiny black specks of dried blood which the fleas excrete, when grooming your cat. To confirm this, wipe them on a moist tissue; if they are droppings they will leave a red smudge.

Most cats with fleas show no adverse reaction, but some are allergic to the flea's saliva and a single bite can set off a very bad skin reaction. Fleas can carry tapeworm larvae, so cats may become infected by swallowing fleas while grooming.

TREATMENT OF ADULT CATS

A flea problem cannot be ignored because the little critters breed so rapidly, particularly in warm weather. Indeed, with the advent of central heating, fleas are present all year round. The adult fleas that are actually on the cat are just the 'tip of the iceberg'. The female lays many eggs in a day, which drop off and contaminate the soft furnishings in your home. They hatch into larvae, then turn into pupae, and finally into adult fleas, which leap onto a passing pet to start the whole life cycle again. Killing adult fleas on the cat is not enough; both your cat and your home must be treated to break the flea life cycle and prevent re-infestation. There are many different flea preparations you can use on your cat, some of which are more effective than others.

producing viable eggs. A small liquid dose is given each month. The active ingredient is absorbed from the gut and is slowly released into the bloodstream over the month. When a flea ingests the ingredient it is effectively sterilized. Any eggs that it lays will not hatch; hence, no new fleas develop. As the adults die off (they only live for seven to fourteen days) the numbers in the household dwindle to nothing. As the product does not kill adult fleas it is necessary to treat the cat with an adult flea killer at the start of the programme.

■ FLEA COLLARS are not always effective and can sometimes cause skin irritation around the neck. It is vital that a flea collar is elasticated so that the cat can wriggle free if the collar becomes caught.

■ INSECTICIDES are available in the form of powders, 'spot-on' preparations and aerosol sprays. Powders aren't always effective and may irritate the cat's airways (and your own) if accidentally inhaled. Products available from veterinary surgeons are more effective than those bought over-the-counter.

Alternative methods of flea control have been used with varying success. These include herbal remedies, garlic and eucalyptus oil and electronic flea traps.

■ ORAL PREPARATIONS are a safe and effective method of flea control, available only from veterinary surgeons. They act by preventing fleas which feed on the treated cat from

PROTECTING THE HOME

■ Vacuum the carpets and the cat's bedding regularly, to reduce the number of flea eggs and pupae present in the home. Placing a flea collar in the vacuum bag will ensure that the fleas do not survive.

■ Special sprays which kill the emerging fleas, or which contain a biological substance that prevents flea eggs from hatching, should be used on carpets, skirting boards and soft furnishings. These are effective for a period of time after application.

TREATMENT OF KITTENS

Young kittens often get infested with fleas, but treatment must be carried out with care. Insecticides should not be used at all on kittens under seven weeks of age; any fleas should be combed out with a fine-toothed 'flea' comb and the kitten's bedding changed

regularly. Pyrethroid powders, or a specific ectoparasiticide (available from your vet) can be used on kittens over seven weeks old, but be sure to follow the manufacturer's directions to the letter.

TICKS

SIGNS AND SYMPTOMS
Cats living in rural areas may pick up sheep ticks in long grass, and urban cats sometimes catch them from hedgehogs. The tick buries its mouth parts deep into the host's skin, where it remains for about five days, feeding on its blood. A bloated tick appears as a grey-blue, pea-sized lump. Because there are usually only one or two ticks on the cat, and because they don't move, they are often mistaken for small cysts. Cats generally seem unperturbed by ticks, but they should be removed as they can transmit diseases.

TREATMENT
The tick's strong mouth parts are used to embed itself in the host with a vice-like grip. It is vital that the tick is made to release its grip before removal, otherwise the mouth parts remain embedded in the skin and will set up infection.

Apply flea spray to the tick (so long as it is not too close to the cat's eyes). The tick will die and drop off within twenty-four hours, or it can be pulled from the skin using tweezers; grasp the dead tick as close to the head as possible, then pull straight up using constant tension. Not a job for the squeamish!

You may find a pump-action flea spray less frightening for your cat than an aerosol spray.

BE CAREFUL

Always take special care when using insecticides on cats; they are susceptible to the toxic effects of chemicals and organophosphate compounds because of their grooming habits. If your cat starts to drool at the mouth shortly after being treated for fleas, he may have been accidentally poisoned. Ring your vet immediately so that an antidote can be administered. Wash off the spray with copious amounts of water.

The following guidelines will help you to tackle the problem of fleas safely:

■ Always follow label directions to the letter and never exceed the recommended dose or frequency of application. This applies whether you are using a prescription-only product or a seemingly innocuous shop-bought product.

■ Spray the cat outside if possible, to avoid inhaling the fumes.

■ Sprays should be directed against the lie of the coat so that the insecticide gets close to the skin rather than staying on the surface.

■ If 'spot-on' insecticide drops are used, they should be applied directly onto the skin, not on the fur. Place the drops between the shoulder blades so that the insecticide cannot be licked off.

■ Do not use flea sprays or other flea products in conjunction with the use of a flea collar. Both contain powerful insecticides, and their combined use may add up to a poisonous dose for a cat.

■ Do not use flea sprays where other domestic or garden insecticides and chemicals are in use at the same time as there could be an adverse chemical interaction. Even fly strips can cause problems.

■ Avoid spraying the cat for a few days after he has received a general anaesthetic, and wait until wounds have healed and stitches have been removed before spraying.

■ Never use disinfectants, or products intended for use against other pests such as flies and garden insects, on your cat.

■ Remove caged birds and cover fish tanks when spraying the room against fleas.

Alternatively, smear the tick with petroleum jelly, which blocks its respiratory pore. Unable to breathe, the tick will die and eventually drop off. A third method is to anaesthetize the tick by swabbing it with alcohol and then tweeze it out, but this can take a good thirty minutes. When the tick is removed, check it under a magnifying glass to make sure the head and mouth parts are intact. Destroy it by burning or by spraying with insecticide.

MANGE

SIGNS AND SYMPTOMS

Mange is a skin disease caused by a microscopic parasite, *Notoedres cati*. It burrows into the cat's skin, causing chronic inflammation, hair loss and irritation, leading to excessive licking and scratching of the affected area. Mange is not common in cats in the United Kingdom.

TREATMENT AND PREVENTION

♦VET Consult a vet if mange is suspected. It is very contagious, so an affected cat must be isolated.

HARVEST MITES

SIGNS AND SYMPTOMS

Commonly known as 'chiggers', these tiny creatures appear as minute orange-red spots on thin-skinned areas between the cat's toes or in the folds of the ears. They cause irritation which makes the cat scratch and bite himself.

TREATMENT AND PREVENTION

Spray with an ordinary flea preparation.

RINGWORM

SIGNS AND SYMPTOMS

In spite of its name, this is a fungal rather than a parasitic condition. The cat may catch it directly from another animal – not necessarily a cat – or indirectly via a contaminated object

WARNING – TRANSMITTABLE

Ringworm is a zoonosis; that is, a disease transmissible between animals and people. Red, circular patches on the forearms are typical signs of human ringworm, and require medical attention. Always wear disposable gloves when handling a cat with ringworm, and wash your hands thoroughly.

such as a feeding bowl. Ringworm in cats does not always produce recognisable symptoms; the only trace of infection may be a few broken hairs and scaly patches on the skin. The head, ears and toes are the most common sites of infection.

TREATMENT AND PREVENTION

♦VET Ringworm is highly contagious and warrants immediate veterinary attention to prevent it spreading further. A vet may be able to confirm a suspected case of ringworm using a device known as a Wood's lamp, although it may be necessary to send off a sample for investigation. He or she will prescribe an antifungal drug called griseofulvin.

The spores of the fungus are very resistant to disinfectants and remain infectious in the household for a long time, therefore drastic measures are necessary to clear the infection.

The cat's bedding must be burned, and all items such as feeding bowls thrown out and replaced. An infected cat should be isolated until treatment is completed (this can take at least a month) and all other cats or dogs in the household should also be treated or infection will spread back and forth between them.

EYE PROBLEMS

Eye problems are relatively rare in cats, but any heavy discharge from the eyes, and any cloudiness or change in colour, should be looked into as it may indicate the presence of infection. If the pupils are enlarged, of differing size or unresponsive to changing levels of light, consult your vet without delay as this may be a symptom of blindness or serious trauma to the head.

CONJUNCTIVITIS

SIGNS AND SYMPTOMS

This is an inflammation of the inside lids of the eye. The insides of the eyelids appear red and inflamed, and the eyes have a watery or mucoid discharge. It usually denotes the onset of cat 'flu (see page 95) but can simply be a bacterial infection, or it may result from a scratch in a fight and in this case only one eye will be affected. Sometimes a foreign body, such as a grass seed, gets into the eye and causes it to become swollen and pus-filled. If this is the case, or an ulcer appears

on the surface of the eye, take the cat to a vet without delay; if left untreated, the ulcer may rupture.

THE THIRD EYELID

The third eyelid, haw or nictitating membrane, is like a tiny shutter at the corner of a cat's eye. It is not normally visible in a healthy cat. Protrusion of the third eyelid across the eye may be a sign of general illness rather than a disease of the eye itself.

TREATMENT AND PREVENTION

♦VET Veterinary treatment is required for this condition. Conjunctivitis is normally treated with medicated ophthalmic drops or ointments to reduce the inflammation.

EAR PROBLEMS

Symptoms of ear trouble include constant shaking of the head and repeated scratching of the ears. The most common cause is ear mites, or it may be that a foreign body, such as a grass seed, has entered the ear and is causing irritation. Never put any liquid in a cat's ear other than prescribed ear drops, and never poke anything into the ear.

EAR MITES

SIGNS AND SYMPTOMS

These tiny mites, smaller than a pin head, live in the ear canal. They cause intense irritation to the skin, resulting in the secretion of a dark brown, pungent wax which is visible on inspection of the inside of the ear. Another tell-tale sign is persistent scratching and shaking of the head.

TREATMENT AND PREVENTION

▶VET Consult a vet, who will clean the ears and prescribe ear drops. These must be applied daily until the dark ear wax has disappeared; this can take about a month because the drops kill the adult mites but not the eggs, and as the eggs hatch out reinfection can occur. Do not exceed the recommended dose as these drops can be toxic to cats. Ear mites are very contagious, so always treat both ears and dose all other animals in the household.

HAEMATOMA

SIGNS AND SYMPTOMS

A haematoma looks like an abscess but is, in fact, a large blood blister. It is caused by trauma, often as the result of a cat fight or excessive scratching, which ruptures blood vessels in the ear flap. Haematomas may be extremely painful and should not be touched.

TREATMENT AND PREVENTION

▶VET Seek immediate veterinary treatment to drain the fluid from the ear. If the haematoma is left untreated the ear will develop a deformity known as flop ear.

MOUTH PROBLEMS

Signs of problems with the mouth and teeth include difficulty in eating, pawing at the mouth, excessive salivation and bad breath. The causes may include inflammation and infection, tooth decay and foreign bodies stuck in the mouth. Older cats with kidney failure may have ulcers in the mouth.

GINGIVITIS

SIGNS AND SYMPTOMS

The presence of dental plaque and hardened tartar caused by bacteria in the mouth leads to bad breath and inflammation of the gums, a condition known as gingivitis. If untreated, the gums will recede, leading eventually to premature tooth loss.

Cats with gingivitis often have a bright red line along the gum margin, and the gums appear red and swollen. Severe cases of gingivitis can also indicate kidney disease (see page 103), feline leukaemia virus (see page 105) or feline immunodeficiency virus (see page 106).

TREATMENT AND PREVENTION

▶VET If you spot signs of gum disease in your cat, seek veterinary treatment before the infection in the mouth gets into the bloodstream. The vet can descale the teeth under anaesthetic. Preventative measures can stop the problem from occuring.

MOUTH ULCERS

▶VET Ulcers on a cat's tongue and gums may be signs of feline respiratory disease (see page 95) or kidney disease (see page 103). Consult a vet for an examination to determine the underlying cause.

If trained from kittenhood, most cats will not object to having their mouths inspected.

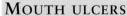

PREVENTATIVE CARE

Cats in the wild keep their teeth and gums healthy by chewing on bones and gristle, but domestic cats fed a diet of soft canned food eventually suffer from a build-up of tartar on their teeth. It is a fact that a surprisingly high percentage of cats over three years old require dental attention. Not only do inflamed gums lead to eventual tooth loss, but bacteria can enter the bloodstream and travel to the various organs within the body, including the heart, liver and kidneys. You can literally add years to your cat's life simply by keeping his teeth healthy.

Research has shown that cats given daily oral care have ninety-five per cent less tartar than those who do not receive any. Ideally, you should encourage a routine of toothbrushing from kittenhood, but even adult cats can be persuaded to 'brush before bedtime' if you have the patience.

■ Use a toothpaste specifically designed for cats and a soft brush or rubber fingertip applicator to gently massage the paste onto the teeth.

■ For those cats who refuse to allow toothbrushing, oral hygiene gels are available in tubes. These are given directly or mixed with food, and most cats seem to like them. They contain natural enzymes which attack existing plaque and retard the formation of new plaque by inhibiting the bacteria responsible for plaque formation.

■ Including chunks of fibrous meat or dry food in the diet will help to exercise the cat's teeth and gums and remove debris.

■ Finally, have your cat's teeth cleaned and polished regularly by a vet, especially when your cat gets older.

Oral hygiene gels are palatable to most cats.

RESPIRATORY PROBLEMS

Signs of respiratory problems include coughing, sneezing and laboured breathing. There may also be a discharge from the eyes and nose. Often these problems are signs of mild illness, and will clear up in a few days. However, some respiratory diseases can be life-threatening, especially in unvaccinated cats, so it is a wise precaution to seek veterinary advice without delay.

FELINE RESPIRATORY DISEASE (CAT 'FLU)

SIGNS AND SYMPTOMS

Cat 'flu is mainly caused by either feline calicivirus (FCV) or feline herpesvirus (FHV) which is also known as feline viral rhinotracheitis (FVR). Cats become infected by breathing in droplets sneezed or coughed out by another cat, and through mutual grooming and shared feeding bowls. The main symptoms of cat 'flu are fever and apathy, followed by sneezing and runny eyes and nose. The cat may refuse to eat because he is unable to smell his food. FHV can cause ulceration of the cornea of the eye; if left untreated, the eyeball may rupture. The FCV virus causes painful mouth ulcers and chronic gingivitis (inflamed gums). Cat 'flu can kill kittens and elderly cats if not treated immediately. Most healthy adult cats have the stamina to recover, but the virus may linger in the body for many years, causing occasional bouts of illness when the cat is

stressed and his defences are lowered. Infected cats can continue to shed the virus and infect other unvaccinated felines for up to eleven months.

TREATMENT AND PREVENTION

▶VET Vaccines are available against cat 'flu. Kittens should be vaccinated at nine and twelve weeks of age, followed by annual boosters. Treatment for infected cats relies on antibiotics to control secondary bacterial infections, multivitamins to build up the cat's resistance, and careful home nursing.

■ The cat should be tempted to eat by serving highly aromatic foods, such as sardines, roast chicken or liver. If this fails, make a broth of meat or chicken and syringe it into the cat's mouth.

■ Clean the cat gently with a cloth and warm water each day as he will not be able to wash himself. Bathe the eyes and nose frequently with a warm solution of salt water (a teaspoon to a pint of water).

■ Placing the cat in a hot, steamy bathroom for an hour each day will help to clear his airways, especially if a decongestant, such as eucalyptus oil, is added to the water.

Both 'flu viruses are fragile: FCV lasts about a week outside the cat and FHV (or FVR) lasts a day. Both are killed by disinfectants.

CHLAMYDIOSIS

SIGNS AND SYMPTOMS

This is caused by Chlamydia, an organism which is a hybrid of a virus and a bacterium. It produces symptoms similar to those of cat 'flu, such as discharges from the eyes and nose. It is not a common infection, and is generally found in multi-cat households. There is a very small risk that this infection could also be transmissible to people, so always wash your hands after handling an infected cat.

TREATMENT AND PREVENTION

♦VET A vaccine may give some protection against the disease. Treatment involves a course of antibiotics. The cat must be isolated from other cats.

LUNGWORMS

SIGNS AND SYMPTOMS

These tiny parasites are sometimes found in cats' lungs, particularly cats in rural areas. It is uncommon and most cats don't show any signs of infestation, though a few may have a persistent, dry cough.

TREATMENT AND PREVENTION

♦VET Affected cats normally get rid of the lungworm parasite of their own accord, but reinfestation often follows. A vet can prescribe drugs to treat lungworm.

DIGESTIVE DISORDERS

The most common problems affecting the cat's digestive system are vomiting, diarrhoea and constipation. Vomiting and diarrhoea may simply be due to a mild tummy upset, but if the symptoms are severe or persist for more than twenty-four hours you should consult a vet without delay. Such symptoms may be due to poisoning or a serious viral infection, both of which are potentially fatal.

FELINE INFECTIOUS ENTERITIS (FIE)

SIGNS AND SYMPTOMS

Also known as feline parvovirus (FPV) and feline panleucopenia, FIE is a highly infectious virus which affects the digestive tract. It can be spread via shared food bowls and litter trays. Most cats contract FIE from a contaminated environment, rather than from infected cats. FIE strikes mainly kittens and younger cats. Unvaccinated older cats are also susceptible, and allowing a cat to get behind with his booster vaccinations may be risky.

Many cats infected with FIE show no clinical signs, and some die very suddenly without presenting any symptoms. Others become acutely ill, but may recover if the disease is detected and treated in time with good nursing and drip feeding.

The initial symptoms of FIE are: fever, vomiting froth and extreme debility. After this stage, profuse, bloody diarrhoea may occur, resulting in serious dehydration. Affected cats often sit hunched over a water or food bowl but unable to drink or eat. A pregnant female can infect her kittens while they are in the womb, killing them or causing cerebellar hypoplasia, a condition that affects the co-ordination and causes tremors.

TREATMENT AND PREVENTION

♦VET A vaccine is available against the disease. It should be given to kittens at nine and twelve weeks and to older cats at any age, with boosters every year. An infected cat will need immediate intravenous fluids and veterinary care, but treatment is not always successful. The entire house must be treated for contamination by FIE virus, which remains infective in the environment for up to a year. Ask your vet to supply an effective decontamination treatment. Since FIE is excreted in the faeces, litter trays should be thoroughly disinfected. Do not introduce a new cat into the household unless it has been vaccinated against the disease at least two weeks previously.

FELINE INFECTIOUS PERITONITIS (FIP)

SIGNS AND SYMPTOMS

Feline infectious peritonitis is a disease which occurs in around ten per cent of cats that are infected with a virus called feline coronavirus (FCoV). FIP can strike cats of any age, sex or breed. The majority of cats will throw off the infection with no clinical signs; others will develop the diseases known as 'wet' and 'dry' FIP, which are fatal.

The FIP virus is spread via contact with infective body excretions or respiratory droplets. It is a fragile virus that quickly dies outside the body, so close contact is required for infection to occur. FIP is difficult to diagnose because the early signs – fever, weight loss, lack of appetite and general debility – are typical of many other diseases. The next signs, which can occur days, weeks or even months later, depend on whether the cat has the dry or the wet form of FIP. In the wet form the abdomen fills up with fluid and appears grossly distended, but the ribs and backbone are prominent. There may also be fluid in the chest, causing difficulty in breathing. The dry form can affect the nervous system, causing convulsions, loss of balance, paralysis or urinary incontinence. If the liver is affected, jaundice may occur. There may also be problems with the eyes, including haemorrhage.

The FIP virus is spread via contact with infective body excretions or respiratory droplets.

TREATMENT AND PREVENTION

Unfortunately, there is no protective vaccine against this disease in the UK, and no cure has yet been found for it. Once the disease is confirmed, it will be only a matter of weeks before death occurs. The virus can be transmitted on food bowls, litter trays, hands, etc., but is killed at room temperature in twenty-four to forty-eight hours, and is destroyed by most household disinfectants. Therefore good hygiene precautions should always be taken. Infected cats must be isolated to prevent the disease from spreading to other cats. Exposure to stray cats should be minimized as a preventative measure. However, other cats in your household will have been exposed to FCoV and need not be segregated and may not go on to develop FIP.

WORMS

Most cats get worms at some point in their lives. Roundworms and tapeworms are the commonest parasites; they live in the stomach and intestine and feed on digested food. These worms rarely produce serious disease, but can lead to a general loss of condition and may cause mild diarrhoea. Your vet can advise you on a regular worming programme to keep your cat free of infestation.

It is important to give the correct drug for the type of parasite infecting the cat. Worming drugs can be bought in pet shops, but they are not as effective as those that your vet can prescribe.

ROUNDWORMS

SIGNS AND SYMPTOMS

If they are passed in the stool, these worms look like small lengths of white thread. Adult cats seldom show any signs of roundworm infection. The problem is more serious in young kittens as the larvae are passed on in the mother's milk if she is infected. Signs include either diarrhoea or constipation, a poor coat, weight loss and a pot-bellied appearance caused by the accumulation of worms and gas in the intestines. Anaemia may well develop, leaving the kitten weakened.

Kittens are far more likely to be infected with roundworm than with tapeworm. Signs may include diarrhoea or a pot-bellied appearance.

TREATMENT AND PREVENTION

▶VET Kittens should be regularly dosed against roundworms (but not tapeworms) from the age of six weeks, following the instructions given by your vet.

TOXOPLASMOSIS

This is caused by a microscopic intestinal parasitic organism, toxoplasma, which often lives in a cat's bowel and sheds its eggs in the cat's motions. Cats become infected by eating contaminated prey or raw meat, but they rarely show signs of illness.

Toxoplasmosis is a zoonosis; a disease which is transmissible to humans (although this one rarely causes illness in adults). Humans may be infected from handling contaminated cat faeces, but you would have to actually swallow the stuff in order to contract the disease – and not many people do that! Infection is far more common from handling or eating infected meat and even uncooked vegetables.

However, in rare cases toxoplasmosis can cause deformity such as blindness in the unborn human foetus. Although the risk is extremely small, it is sensible for pregnant women to avoid handling garden soil where a cat may have defecated (and it is a good excuse to hand over litter tray duties to someone else!). Thanks to scare stories in the press, pregnant women are sometimes advised to get rid of a much-loved family cat because of the perceived risk from toxoplasmosis. As long as the above precautions are taken, this is quite unnecessary.

TAPEWORMS

SIGNS AND SYMPTOMS

These are flat, tape-like worms that will attach themselves to the wall of the gut. They can grow up to 60 cm long and consist of egg-filled segments that break off and are passed out with the motions. The tapeworm segments disintegrate, releasing the eggs. The eggs are then eaten by rodents. The cycle is completed when this host is eaten by a cat. The most common hosts are fleas, which are sometimes swallowed during grooming. Cats can be infested with tapeworms without showing any symptoms apart from a mild tummy upset. If your cat is suffering from tapeworm, you will nearly always notice segments (they look like small grains of rice) in the motions or crusted under the cat's tail.

TREATMENT AND PREVENTION

All adult cats should be wormed routinely against roundworms and tapeworms every six months. Kittens under six months old must not be dosed against tapeworm except under veterinary supervision. If a cat is kept clear of fleas he is unlikely to catch the most common type of tapeworm. Tapeworms cannot be passed directly from cat to cat, nor can people pick one up from a cat.

FUR BALLS

SIGNS AND SYMPTOMS

When cats groom themselves they may ingest loose hairs which accumulate in the stomach to form a matted ball. Usually fur balls are regurgitated or passed through the bowels, but in bad cases they may cause an obstruction in the bowel. Signs of fur ball include a low, crouching cough, with the head and neck outstretched, and a pronounced swallowing action. Some cats eat grass to aid the process of eliminating fur balls. Successful vomiting produces a tightly-packed sausage-shaped bundle of fur.

TREATMENT AND PREVENTION
Try dosing the cat with olive oil or butter, or give a meal of oily fish which will soften any fur balls and allow them to be passed out.

Proprietary fur ball remedies are also available. The prevention is to groom your cat regularly so there is less fur to be swallowed.

DIARRHOEA

SIGNS AND SYMPTOMS
Occasional bouts of diarrhoea may be caused by stress, an abrupt change in diet, or by drinking too much milk. Consult a vet if the

diarrhoea persists for longer than twenty-four hours or if it is accompanied by vomiting or blood in the faeces. These may be signs of a serious bacterial infection or poisoning.

TREATMENT AND PREVENTION
Give the affected cat plenty to drink to prevent dehydration. An adult cat with diarrhoea should be starved for

A little olive oil or butter will help your cat to pass fur balls.

twenty-four hours. After this, give boiled fish or chicken but no milk or red meat for the next three days, until the cat's stomach settles. A teaspoonful of natural yogurt with food helps to colonize the intestine with beneficial bacteria.

CONSTIPATION

SIGNS AND SYMPTOMS

This may be due to a number of causes, including fur balls, and is fairly common in elderly cats. A constipated cat will appear lethargic and will strain on his litter tray without passing a motion.

♦VET It is important to be sure that it is faeces that the cat is trying to pass; if it is unable to pass urine, this is an emergency situation requiring immediate veterinary attention (see page 103).

TREATMENT AND PREVENTION

Minor cases can be dealt with by feeding oily fish, such as canned sardines or pilchards, or adding a little butter and some bran to the cat's food. There are veterinary preparations for really stubborn cases.

As a cat gets older he is more likely to suffer from problems like diarrhoea or constipation. Careful attention to diet and grooming will reduce your cat's chances of falling ill.

URINARY TRACT PROBLEMS

Urinary problems are quite common in cats, particularly as they get older. Although it can be difficult with a cat who normally toilets outside, you should try to check that he urinates normally. All urinary tract disorders are serious and potentially life-threatening, so if you notice your cat straining unproductively, don't wait until the morning; contact your vet immediately.

FELINE UROLOGICAL SYNDROME (FUS)

SIGNS AND SYMPTOMS

This condition is also known as feline lower urinary tract disease (FLUTD) or urolithiasis. FUS is caused by a build-up of crystals called struvite which blocks the urethra, obstructing the flow of urine. The problem is more common in males, particularly neuters, because they have narrower urethras than females. The cat strains frequently to pass small drops of urine, or cannot pass any at all. Normally clean cats sometimes urinate around the house. Other symptoms can include depression, loss of appetite and persistent licking around the urethral opening. It is important not to confuse these symptoms with constipation as urethral obstruction is an emergency situation requiring immediate veterinary attention. When urine cannot be passed, the bladder soon fills up to capacity and back pressure on the kidneys can quickly lead to kidney failure.

The underlying cause of FUS is not fully understood, but many factors have been implicated, such as obesity, lack of exercise, dietary factors and not drinking enough water. Also, struvite formation is more likely if the urine is too alkaline (a cat's urine should be acid).

TREATMENT AND PREVENTION

♦VET The vet will try to unblock the urethra and empty the bladder. Cats usually respond well to a course of antibiotics and urinary acidifiers, but the problem has a tendency to recur. Cats that develop recurrent urinary problems are often overweight, neutered males with a sedentary lifestyle. Try to encourage the cat to be more active and eat a weight-reducing diet. Avoid giving dry foods, and encourage drinking by making fresh water available at all times and offering milk, gravy and other palatable liquids. Urinary acidifiers which come in a palatable powder form can be sprinkled on the cat's food, and special diets are available which produce an acid urine and are lower in certain minerals associated with struvite formation.

CHRONIC KIDNEY FAILURE

SIGNS AND SYMPTOMS

This is the most significant problem that affects older cats. The disease progresses very slowly and early signs are often not noticeable. As the kidney function deteriorates through wear and tear, the cat shows an increased desire to urinate coupled with increased thirst. As the disease progresses, urea builds up in the bloodstream and causes bad breath, vomiting and ulcers on the tongue. The cat is very thin and depressed, refusing all food. At the very end the urea level may affect the brain, causing fits.

TREATMENT AND PREVENTION

▸VET It is important to get treatment as soon as the signs start; if left too long, irreversible damage will be done to the kidneys. Diagnosis is made by a blood test. Sadly, therapy cannot reverse the condition; it can only slow its progression.

■ Most importantly, a constant supply of clean drinking water must be available at all times to satisfy increased thirst and to stimulate the kidneys to function.

■ The cat should be given a low-protein diet so as to decrease the burden on the kidneys and reduce the level of toxins in the system. Special low-protein diets are available from veterinary surgeons, though not all cats like these.

■ You could try feeding a home-made diet consisting of a little fish, chicken, cooked egg or cottage cheese, along with carbohydrates, such as rice or pasta, and fat.

■ The vet will give injections of anabolic steroids which help to build up body weight. Dietary management will also help.

Check your cat whenever possible for any signs of difficulty in passing urine.

■ You should also supplement the cat's vitamin intake, on veterinary advice, since the high urine output results in a loss of water-soluble vitamins, especially the B group.

CYSTITIS

SIGNS AND SYMPTOMS

Inflammation of the bladder, or cystitis, is a painful condition which produces similar symptoms to FUS (on page 103). It is commonly caused by a bacterial infection and may be associated with struvite formation. It is quite common in female cats, particularly tortoiseshells. Signs include frequent urination and straining and an increased thirst. The urine may be blood-stained and the cat may persistently lick his rear end. Some affected cats will start to urinate in abnormal sites around the house.

TREATMENT AND PREVENTION

▸VET The cat will need a course of antibiotics for at least a week to remove all the bacteria which cause the cystitis. Pooling of urine in the bladder for many hours encourages the growth of bacteria and contributes towards cystitis. Therefore it is important that a cat is never left indoors without a litter tray. Special diets may be necessary in recurrent cases.

BLOOD AND GLANDULAR DISORDERS

A number of viruses can infect the cat, some of which attack the immune system or the bone marrow where red blood cells are produced, causing serious illness such as anaemia and cancer. To keep the immune system primed and help it to fight against viral infection, your cat should be given routine vaccinations, good nutrition, and be protected as much as possible from contact with stray cats. Glandular disorders such as hyperthyroidism are generally associated with older cats.

FELINE LEUKAEMIA VIRUS (FeLV)

SIGNS AND SYMPTOMS

Feline leukaemia is a serious long-term disease which in some cases damages the cat's immune system, leaving him susceptible to recurrent infections of the mouth, chest, skin and bladder. It can also cause anaemia, and some cats develop cancer. There is a long incubation period (months to years) from infection with FeLV to development of disease, though the cat is still infectious. A cat does not die of FeLV, but of whatever illness it develops due to the breakdown of the immune system.

The virus is found in the saliva of infected cats and dies rapidly once outside the body so it can only be spread by close contact with an infected cat, via mating, biting, mutual grooming or shared food bowls. Kittens between six weeks and four months old, and those infected before birth, are particularly susceptible to infection by FeLV. Of these, most will die within two to five years. After the age of four months, most cats produce antibodies to the virus and recover from the infection. These cats will have a life-long immunity to FeLV, although this resistance can be overcome by large doses of the virus (for example, through prolonged contact with an infected cat). FeLV does not infect humans or other animals.

TREATMENT AND PREVENTION

Although vaccines are available, they are not 100 per cent effective in every case. There is no effective treatment for FeLV. Treatment is supportive, geared towards the associated symptoms as they arise.

■ Any cat which has a poor health record of persistent infections, or signs of anaemia, should be blood-tested for the virus. All cats that test positive must be isolated or euthanased to prevent infection spreading to other cats.

■ An FeLV positive cat should not be introduced into a multi-cat household, even if the resident cats are vaccinated (unless you are certain that they have developed natural immunity).

■ FeLV is a fragile virus and does not survive for long on hands, bowls and so on. It is easily killed by any disinfectant.

FELINE IMMUNODEFICIENCY VIRUS (FIV)

SIGNS AND SYMPTOMS

This virus causes symptoms similar to those caused by the FeLV virus (see above), namely anaemia and chronic recurring infections, but it is not known to produce tumours. The most commonly reported sign of FIV is gingivitis. Many FIV-positive cats can remain healthy for years before secondary infections become apparent.

The virus is present in the blood and saliva of infected cats. It is a fragile virus and dies very quickly outside the body, so cannot be transmitted indirectly. Transmission appears to be mainly through deep bite wounds. FIV is most prevalent in feral, entire toms who get into a lot of fights. FIV is seen more commonly in cats slightly older than typical FeLV cases (the average is about five years). It should be stressed that FIV cannot be transmitted to humans or other animals.

TREATMENT AND PREVENTION

A blood test is available to diagnose FIV. An infected cat which is given to fighting should be isolated to prevent him from spreading the disease to other cats. No vaccine currently exists. Treatment is merely supportive, geared towards the FIV-associated diseases as they arise.

■ Keeping your cat indoors at night is a preventative measure as this is when most cat fights occur.

■ Oil of evening primrose has been shown to have a beneficial effect on FIV-positive cats.

ANAEMIA

SIGNS/SYMPTOMS

Anaemia refers to a shortage of red blood cells circulating within the bloodstream, which reduces the amount of oxygen carried in the blood. Signs of anaemia include pale eye and mouth membranes, lethargy, breathlessness and loss of appetite. Anaemic cats often eat earth or other unnatural materials. Apart from chronic kidney disease and Feline Leukaemia Virus (FeLV), the main causes of anaemia are:

■ FELINE INFECTIOUS ANAEMIA (**FIA**) This is a severe form of anaemia caused by an infectious blood parasite, Haemobartonella felis, that destroys red blood cells. It is transmitted by blood-sucking parasites such as fleas and ticks. A blood test will reveal the presence of the parasite, which can be killed with a course of antibiotics; the prognosis for the cat is good. Unfortunately, however, FIA often occurs where there is a concurrent Feline Leukaemia condition (see page 105) and in this case the prognosis is very poor.

■ HAEMORRHAGE This is loss of blood due to an accident, a constantly bleeding ulcer or tumour, or ingestion of a rodent poison which prevents blood clotting. If this is the case, seek veterinary help at once.

TREATMENT

♦VET Anaemia is difficult to diagnose but can be confirmed by a blood test. Treatment involves identifying and curing the underlying cause of the problem, combined with iron supplements and, in severe cases, blood transfusions.

HYPERTHYROIDISM

SIGNS AND SYMPTOMS

This disease is only found in older cats (nine years and over). It is caused by a benign tumour on the thyroid gland at the base of the throat, which causes excessive secretion of thyroid hormone. The heart rate soars and the cat becomes hyperactive and loses weight in spite of an increased appetite. Fluid intake and urine output may also be increased. Other signs include trembling, intolerance of heat, nervousness and panting.

TREATMENT AND PREVENTION

♦VET The problem can be diagnosed with blood tests, and treated either by removing the growth or by giving drugs that reduce the output of thyroid hormone and control the heart rate.

DIABETES MELLITUS

SIGNS AND SYMPTOMS

This is commonly known as sugar diabetes. It is caused by inadequate production of insulin by the pancreas. Cats with diabetes are often overweight at first but then lose weight as the condition progresses. There is increased urine production and a corresponding increase in thirst. Sometimes it is possible to detect a smell like nail varnish remover on the breath.

TREATMENT

♦VET The condition can be diagnosed with a blood or urine test. Treatment involves dietary control and regular injections of insulin.

THE ELDERLY CAT

'The beautiful cat endures and endures.' **Grave inscription (Thebes)**

Kittens develop rapidly during the first two years of their lives, and after this the ageing process slows down and the average cat will not show any signs of age until he is over ten years old. The average

lifespan of a cat is fourteen to sixteen years, although nowadays it is not uncommon to encounter cats in their early twenties, thanks to advances in feline nutrition and veterinary medicine.

After the age of about fourteen, a cat must be considered to be elderly and should be treated with the care and respect his advanced years have earned him. You will probably notice him slowing down gradually, spending longer periods asleep. Try not to disturb his daily routine and ensure that he has a comfortable bed in a quiet corner, away from draughts. A covered hot-water bottle or a heated pad, designed specially for pets, is useful if your cat feels the cold or is recovering from an illness. An indoor litter tray will be welcomed in wet or cold weather even if your cat normally goes outdoors for his toilet.

Some older cats call out at night when the house is quiet as they feel lonely or in need of reassurance. Placing the cat's bed in your own bedroom may solve this. Alternatively, place something that bears your scent, such as an old pullover, in the cat's bed. A radio playing at low volume will provide company.

With age, the joints and muscles become a little stiff and your cat will appreciate a helping hand with his grooming. Encourage him to play the occasional game to keep the joints mobile and the muscles toned.

HEALTH CARE

In common with old people, the cat is liable to suffer from various complaints including tooth decay, failing eyesight and hearing, constipation, urinary problems, arthritis, heart and chest complaints – the list is depressingly long! But cats are very resilient creatures and will muddle along quite nicely, thank you. You can certainly help by arranging for your mature cat to have a veterinary check-up once or twice a year; this way, any degenerative problems can be diagnosed and treated in their early stages, possibly prolonging your cat's life for months or even years. Watch out for any signs of abnormal behaviour that might indicate the onset of disease. In particular, a sudden increase in thirst or loss of weight is cause for concern as these may indicate kidney failure or urinary tract disorders (see page 103), so have your cat checked out without delay.

FEEDING

As a cat gets older, his digestive system becomes less efficient and he requires several smaller meals a day rather than two main meals. Because his sense of smell and taste are diminished he may become more finicky about his food, so indulge him with titbits of strong-smelling, nourishing and easily digested foods, such as chicken and sardines. You may also find that he will accept food from your fingers which he will not eat from a dish.

If your cat is becoming overweight, feed him one of the formulated rations aimed

KATIE

Ten-year-old Katie was homed to Colin and Jane Weaver who live near Huntingdon, Cambridgeshire, having been rescued as a kitten by the Peterborough Branch of the CPL. She had been found on a farm and was terrified of dogs. With a lot of patience Colin won her over and she has been devoted to him ever since. Katie perches high on his chest whilst he is sitting relaxing and she has a deep-throated purr which sends shivers down your spine. As a kitten she was incurably nosey and got into all sorts of scrapes, such as getting shut in cupboards. Now she rules the other two cats in the household in a queenly fashion. She knows she is superior, and that's all there is to it.

specifically at older and less active cats, which contain more fibre and less fat. Sardines in oil once or twice a week will help to prevent constipation, a condition to which elderly cats are prone.

Always provide your cat with easy access to fresh water. This will encourage frequent urination and help to decrease the risk of feline urological syndrome (see page 103). If he doesn't like water, give him meat broth or fish soup to increase his liquid intake.

EUTHANASIA

Hopefully your cat will simply pass away peacefully in his sleep when his time comes but unfortunately this is often not the case. If your

cat is in great pain that cannot be relieved and is obviously suffering, then the final kindness you can offer is to allow him a dignified end. It is a difficult and distressing decision, but in the end it is not the length of a cat's life that matters, but the quality of his life.

When the time comes, the vet will inject the cat with an overdose of an anaesthetic drug. The cat passes away in a few seconds with no signs of distress. You can choose whether or not to stay by your cat's side at the end; if you do so, try not to show any distress so as not to upset your pet. Gently stroke him, giving comfort and reassurance.

Most vets can arrange cremation or burial for your pet, or you may prefer to bury him in your back garden or in a pet cemetery.

Losing a pet can be extremely traumatic, particularly when he has shared your life for many years. Don't feel embarrassed about expressing your grief; you will find it

A great many cats these days reach their teens and twenties with little or no sign of deterioration. Well, perhaps a touch of middle-age spread.

An older cat will appreciate something in his bed that contains your scent to prevent him feeling lonely at night in a quiet house.

enormously helpful to talk it through with an understanding friend. In recognition of the very real bond that exists between people and their pets, some veterinary practices now have pet-loss counsellors on hand to assist you in your time of need. You may find some solace in making a donation to an animal charity in memory of your pet, or in planting a rose bush or a tree in his favourite spot in the garden. Allow yourself time to reflect on the good times you and your cat have shared over the years.

CHAPTER FIVE

FIRST AID

First Aid is the emergency care given to a cat suffering injury
or illness of sudden onset.

AIMS OF FIRST AID

1 Keep the animal alive.
2 Prevent unnecessary suffering.
3 Prevent further injury.

RULES OF FIRST AID

KEEP CALM.
If you panic you will be unable to help effectively.

CONTACT A VET AS SOON AS POSSIBLE.
Advice given over the telephone may be life-saving.

AVOID INJURY TO YOURSELF.
A distressed or injured animal may bite.

CONTROL HAEMORRHAGE.
Excessive blood loss can lead to severe shock and death.

MAINTAIN AN AIRWAY.
Failure to breathe or obtain adequate oxygen can lead to brain damage or
loss of life within five minutes (see artificial respiration).

COMMON ACCIDENTS AND EMERGENCIES

The following common accidents and emergencies all require
First Aid action. In an emergency, your priorities are to keep the cat
alive and comfortable until he can be examined by a vet. In many
cases, there is effective action that you can take immediately to
help preserve your cat's health and life.

FIRST AID

Cats are reputed to have nine lives. Unfortunately this is not nearly enough for some of them. While their speed, agility and highly-tuned senses get cats out of a lot of trouble, their natural curiosity lands them in plenty more. In an emergency situation, some basic knowledge of first aid, such as how to control bleeding, treat shock and restart breathing, could mean the difference between life and death to your cat. This section lists some of the more common emergencies that occur with cats and gives advice on how to deal with them and help your cat get back on the road to recovery.

As soon as a wound is discovered, bathe it immediately to reduce the risk of an abscess forming under the skin.

BITES

By far the most common veterinary problem in cats is infected fight wounds. When cats bite each other during a fight, bacteria from their mouths is introduced into the resulting wound. A puncture wound may be almost invisible on the surface but often penetrates deep into the flesh. If the skin heals over while the flesh beneath is still infected, an abscess will form in a few days. Once an abscess has come to a head and burst it will leave a gaping hole that must be kept clean to prevent reinfection, and a course of antibiotics will be necessary. In severe cases the wound may require stitching.

IF THE BITE WOUND IS DISCOVERED

There is less danger of this occurring if the bite wound is discovered in time and kept open until the discharge has ceased.

■ TREATMENT: bathe the wound at frequent intervals with a wad of cotton wool which is soaked in a solution of a teaspoonful of salt to 300 ml/½ pint warm water. Gently press around the wound to release any pus.

IF THE BITE WOUND IS NOT DISCOVERED

If the initial bite is not discovered and kept open, a painful abscess can develop with surprising rapidity, leaving the cat feeling unwell and with a high temperature. Often

RESTRAINING A CAT

A difficult cat can be restrained by either:
1 Holding the scruff of his neck and front legs so the cat can be held firmly down.
2 Initially holding him by the scruff of his neck then wrapping him up in a towel or coat.

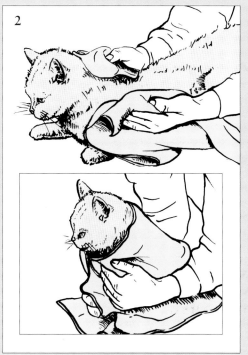

the owner is unaware that there is an abscess as it is hidden beneath the fur, and is puzzled and anxious when their cat, who was fine just a short time ago, suddenly appears subdued and refuses to eat for no apparent reason.

■ TREATMENT: if you find an abscess, do not attempt to lance it. The cat should be taken to your vet, who will open and drain the abscess and prescribe a course of antibiotics to control infection.

CHOKING

If you notice your cat retching and pawing at his mouth, he may have an object lodged in his mouth or throat, and immediate action is necessary. Retching may have other causes, such as infection or fur balls. Seek veterinary advice if it persists.

■ TREATMENT: restrain the cat by wrapping him in a towel and remove the object, preferably with a pair of tweezers. If this is unsuccessful, seek veterinary help immediately.

■ PREVENTION: if you give your cat fresh fish or chicken, always make sure that any bones are removed as they are small and sharp and can cause choking. Never leave a threaded sewing needle lying around as you can bet your life your cat will find it, play with it and possibly eat it, and it may become lodged across the hard palate between the back teeth or in the throat.

LAMENESS

Limping and lameness may have one of several causes. In older cats, lameness may be due to arthritis and will be of gradual onset. If the lameness appears suddenly, check for any abnormal swelling on the leg which may indicate a sprain or an infected bite or wound. If the leg is held at an odd angle there may be a fracture or dislocation. Examine the paws for signs of any foreign material such as broken glass or a thorn, either in the paw pad or between the toes. Seeds and splinters are difficult to see but can be very painful to the cat.

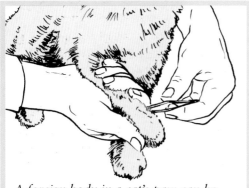

A foreign body in a cat's paw can be removed with tweezers but if it is embedded in the paw pad consult a vet.

■ TREATMENT: If you suspect a fracture or dislocation, consult your vet immediately; the cat could have been in accident and may be in shock or have internal injuries. Foreign material will need to be removed by the vet if you cannot do it; seeds and splinters can work their way right up the leg, eventually creating an abscess elsewhere.

STINGS

Flying insects are irresistible to kittens in particular, and the commonest sites for stings are on the paws and mouth.

■ TREATMENT: if a sting is visible remove it with tweezers. Bee stings should be bathed with a weak solution of bicarbonate of soda: one teaspoon per cup of water. Wasp stings should be bathed with vinegar.

Most stings are not serious and the swelling should subside after a few hours. If your cat has been stung in the mouth or throat, however, you must seek urgent veterinary help as the throat is liable to swell rapidly and cause asphyxiation.

BURNS

If a cat has been burned or scalded it is essential to act immediately.

■ TREATMENT: cool down the skin as quickly as possible by running copious amounts of cold water over the area for several minutes. Never apply butter or skin cream to a burn as this will only increase the inflammation. Unless the burn is very minor, seek veterinary assistance as soon as possible.

POISONING

Thanks to their careful eating habits, cats are very rarely poisoned. But if they do ingest poison the results can be serious as cats cannot metabolize certain substances that do not harm other species.

■ TREATMENT: if you suspect poisoning,

POISONOUS SUBSTANCES

Some of the more common substances that are poisonous to cats include:

RODENTICIDES

The most likely source of poisoning in cats comes from rodenticides and poisoned bait, used to control rats and mice. The cat may be poisoned either directly by swallowing the bait, or by eating a poisoned rodent. Coma is induced by the rat poison alphachloralose, and death can result from hypothermia as the body temperature drops. It is vital to keep the victim warm using covered hot-water bottles while veterinary help is sought. Spontaneous haemorrhaging is caused by the rat poison Warfarin; blood may appear in the faeces and urine, and there may be small red patches on the gums. This poison is treatable with daily injections of vitamin K.

MEDICINES

Under no circumstances should you give human medicines to cats as they cannot metabolize certain compounds which are harmless to us. Never give aspirin to a cat except under veterinary supervision. Only very small doses may be used for specific conditions. An excess causes convulsions, severe vomiting and diarrhoea. It will also damage the liver, and it should never be given if the liver is impaired. Similarly, antiseptic creams or lotions based on phenol or cresol are toxic and should never be applied to wounds.

GARDEN CHEMICALS

Certain plants, both indoor and outdoor, are poisonous, but most cats are too fastidious to eat any that are harmful. Accidental poisoning is, however, possible if a cat has chewed grass or plants that have been treated with an insecticide or weedkiller, causing symptoms such as convulsions, vomiting and foaming at the mouth.

If eaten by a cat, slug pellets containing metaldehyde will cause fits, loss of balance, salivation and twitching, and its eyes dart from side to side. Always purchase the more modern type of slug pellets which contain substances that repel animals. Even better, use 'green' methods of slug control such as sinking jars of beer or milk in the earth around your plants.

Wood preservatives such as creosote and tar are also highly poisonous. If you are treating sheds and fences, make sure you choose one of the non-poisonous preservatives that are now available.

Always mop up any spills of anti-freeze on your drive or in your garage. Some cats are actually attracted to the stuff, and if ingested it causes convulsions and sometimes coma and death.

contact your vet immediately and, if possible advising him of the name of the poison concerned. Specific antidotes are available for some poisons, and the earlier the antidote can be administered the better. Do not attempt any first aid until you have spoken to the vet as the treatment will depend on the nature of the poison involved.

■ CAUTION: do not attempt to induce vomiting except under veterinary advice as

Wrapping the cat in a towel should make your task easier.

emetics are not recommended for all poisons. In any case, emetics are only of use if the cat has been seen to eat the poison within the previous half-hour. If this is the case, and the vet has advised it, the cat can safely be made to vomit by doing the following:

1 Use a strong salt solution, or one crystal of washing soda administered like a tablet (see page 85 for how to give tablets). Vomiting will occur within ninety seconds.

2 Keep the cat warm and quiet and handle him as little as possible until he can be taken to a vet. In all cases of poisoning do not

give any food for at least twenty-four hours.
NOTE: when grooming themselves, cats may accidentally ingest toxic substances such as paint, tar or petrol that have contaminated their coat or their paws. If this happens, do the following:

1 First wrap the cat in a towel, if necessary, to prevent him from licking his coat.

2 Wash the offending substance from the cat immediately, using copious amounts of water. Never use solvents, such as turpentine, to remove oily or sticky substances from a cat's coat as these are very toxic. Use either a waterless cleansing agent, washing up liquid, petroleum jelly, butter or vegetable oil and wash it off using warm water and a mild shampoo.

STARVATION

Cats sometimes accidentally get shut in a garden shed or garage when they have been exploring. They have been known to survive for up to six weeks without food or water. If you find such a cat in a collapsed state, consult a vet immediately.

■ TREATMENT: if the cat is conscious, start by feeding small quantities of water. If the cat is able to keep this down, follow up with glucose or honey in water, or a proprietary liquid food (available from a vet). Light solid foods such as boiled chicken or white fish can be offered after a day or two.

If you or your neighbours have cats, it is always worth checking your garden shed or garage before you lock the door behind you as cats tend to slip in silently without you noticing.

KITTENING PROBLEMS

The cat is one of the most attentive of mothers and usually has no problems in delivering her brood efficiently. Nevertheless it is wise to monitor the birth (from a discreet distance) because an inexperienced queen can occasionally be confused as to what to do with the kittens. Do not interfere if there are no problems to allow bonding.

1 Be prepared with clean towels, a bowl of boiled water, some sterilized cotton thread and blunt-tipped scissors, just in case there is a hiccup in the proceedings.

2 Labour normally takes one or two hours for the first kitten to arrive, and they are usually born at intervals of about twenty minutes. Check that an afterbirth is delivered with each kitten, as if one is retained within the mother it can cause serious infection.

3 If the mother seems distressed or has been straining for more than 30 minutes between births without producing a kitten, veterinary help should be sought urgently as a kitten may have become trapped.

If a kitten appears stuck halfway out, you need to act quickly. Wash your hands and gently grasp the kitten behind the ears and pull very gently outwards and downwards in an arc, preferably at the same time as the mother is bearing down, whilst very gently and slowly rotating the kitten first to the left and then to the right, not more than about thirty degrees.

4 Once a kitten is born the mother will bite through the umbilical cord to release the kitten from its placenta. She then nips open the amniotic sac covering the kitten and washes the kitten with her rough tongue to stimulate it to breathe. If for some reason the mother ignores the kitten, you will have to substitute these tasks. Pull off the amniotic sac and clear the kitten's mouth and nostrils of mucus to allow it to breathe. When it is breathing, use sterilized cotton thread and scissors to tie and cut the umbilical cord about 7 cm (3 in) from the navel, squeezing the cord immediately below the point at which it is severed to stem the blood flow and help the end of the cord to clot and close. If the mother is not attentive, rub the kitten vigorously with a towel and encourage it to suckle.

ACCIDENTS AND EMERGENCY CARE

ROAD ACCIDENTS

If you suspect that your cat has been hit by a vehicle, the most obvious sign to look for is broken, split claws caused by digging them into the road at the moment of impact. Other signs are fresh dirt or oil in the coat, bleeding from anywhere on the body, pale gums and cold paws. Contact your vet immediately, particularly if there are large wounds or heavy bleeding, if the cat's breathing is distressed or if he is in pain. Even if your cat seems relatively unscathed there may be internal injuries which you cannot see. In the meantime keep him warm as he may be in shock. (See the following pages for further advice on first aid and moving an injured cat.)

FALLS

Cats usually manage to land safely on their feet after a fall. However, they do sometimes land on their chin, too, and this can lead to fractures of the jaw or the roof of the mouth. There is also the possibility of concussion or internal injury, so contact your vet if you know that your cat has had a fall.

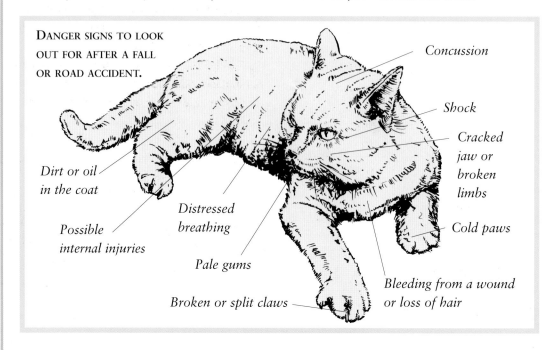

DANGER SIGNS TO LOOK OUT FOR AFTER A FALL OR ROAD ACCIDENT.

Concussion

Shock

Cracked jaw or broken limbs

Cold paws

Bleeding from a wound or loss of hair

Broken or split claws

Pale gums

Distressed breathing

Possible internal injuries

Dirt or oil in the coat

DROWNING

Fortunately, drowning is extremely rare as cats do not like water, but accidents do happen. If the cat is motionless after he has been pulled from the water, the first thing to do is to drain the water from his lungs.

■ TREATMENT: hold the cat upside down by his hind legs, gripping above the hock joints, and swing him gently up in front of you and then down between your legs. Continue swinging him back and forth, holding him well clear of the ground. If the cat is still not breathing he should be laid on his side and his chest pressed rapidly several times (see Artificial Respiration, page 123). Keep the mouth open and pull the tongue forward to assist breathing. Keep the cat warm and seek veterinary help.

MOVING AN INJURED CAT

If you come across an injured cat, try to move him as little as possible except to get him to a place of safety. To prevent causing further injury, avoid twisting or bending the cat's body.

■ IF THE CAT IS UNCONSCIOUS OR UNABLE TO MOVE

1 Find something rigid, such as a board or a tray, or, failing that, a blanket or coat, to use as an improvised stretcher.

2 Gently coax one hand under the shoulders and one under the rump to distribute the cat's weight evenly and slide him onto the stretcher.

3 Ensure that the airway is clear and pull the tongue forward.

4 If necessary, try to stop any severe bleeding (see page 125).

5 Support the head just a little lower than the rest of the body, without allowing it to dangle; this will encourage the flow of blood to the brain and prevent brain damage.

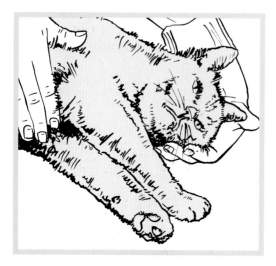

■ IF THE CAT IS CONSCIOUS

An injured cat that is conscious will be in a state of shock and may try to scratch or bite, so approach him very slowly and cautiously.

1 Pick him up by the scruff of the neck while supporting the rump and place him in a suitable carrier or a strong cardboard box.

2 If the cat struggles violently, cover him with a blanket or towel to restrain him. Wear gloves to protect your hands if possible.

3 Keep the cat wrapped up and warm to prevent shock (see opposite) and take him to a vet immediately (get someone to telephone the surgery to warn them in advance that you are on the way). Consult your doctor if you get bitten or scratched deeply as these wounds can quickly turn septic.

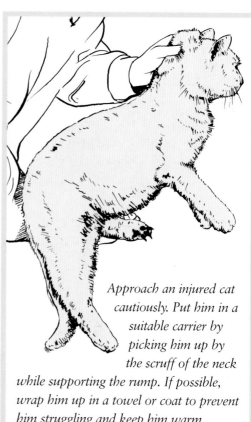

Approach an injured cat cautiously. Put him in a suitable carrier by picking him up by the scruff of the neck while supporting the rump. If possible, wrap him up in a towel or coat to prevent him struggling and keep him warm.

SHOCK

A cat may go into a state of shock following a road accident, dog attack or similar trauma.

■ **SYMPTOMS**

■ The cat will appear weak and shaky and his breathing and pulse will be rapid.

■ He may feel cold to the touch and the linings of the mouth and eyes will be pale.

■ **TREATMENT:** it is vital to keep the cat warm by wrapping him in a blanket or towel. Aluminium foil and plastic 'bubble' wrapping material make excellent insulators. Lay the cat down with his head slightly lower than the rest of his body to help blood to reach the brain. Seek veterinary help immediately.

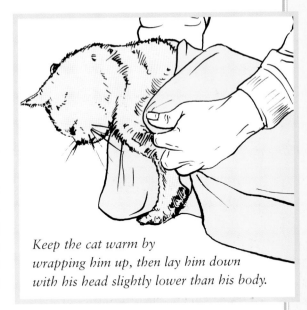

Keep the cat warm by wrapping him up, then lay him down with his head slightly lower than his body.

ARTIFICIAL RESPIRATION

In an emergency, if a cat suffers respiratory failure it is possible to attempt artificial respiration on him, though this must be done immediately if the cat is to survive.

1 Lay the cat on one side with his head tilted downwards.

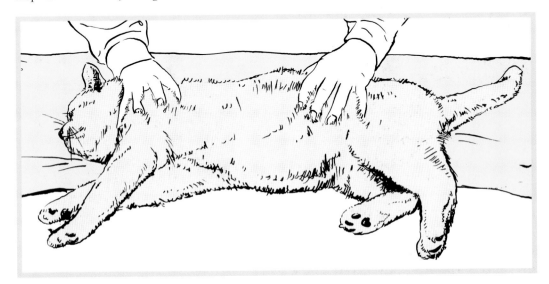

2 Open the mouth and ensure that the airway is clear.

3 Pull the tongue forward to clear the throat. This may be enough to stimulate breathing, causing the cat to regain consciousness.

4 If the cat remains unconscious, attempt to stimulate breathing manually. Lay the cat on his right side and place your hands, one on top of the other, on the chest behind the shoulder.

5 Press down rapidly several times. Repeat every five seconds until the cat breathes.

6 Alternatively, try using the mouth-to-nose method. Tilt back the cat's head, hold the mouth shut and blow into both nostrils for two to three seconds to inflate the lungs.

7 Wait until air is expelled, then repeat until the cat starts to breathe on his own. If there is no response after two or three minutes, cardiac massage is needed.

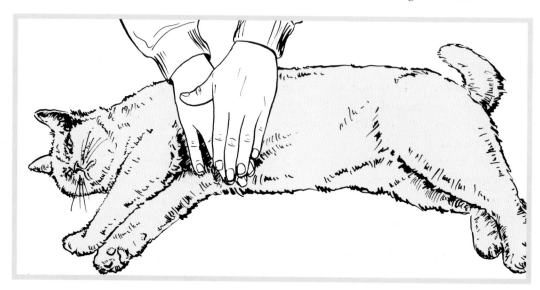

CARDIAC MASSAGE

1 Press the chest, behind the elbow, using fingers and thumb.

2 Repeat twice a second until the heart can be felt beating again.

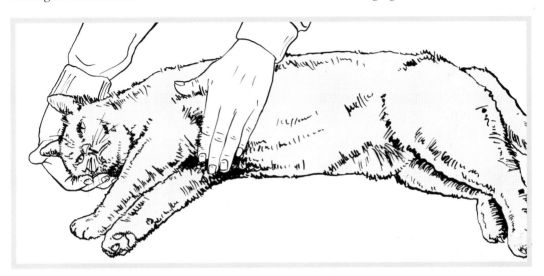

STOPPING BLEEDING

If there is external bleeding from a wound the first step is to stop the bleeding as quickly as possible.

■ TREATMENT

1 Apply pressure to the wound with a wad of gauze or cotton soaked in cold water (do not use cotton wool as the fibres may stick to open wounds).

2 Maintain pressure for two or three minutes to stop the bleeding.

3 A bandage may then be wrapped firmly over the dressing to hold it in place.

NOTE: seek urgent veterinary attention if the bleeding is severe or prolonged.

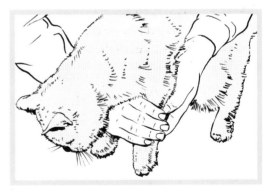

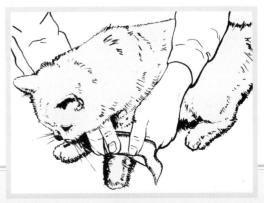

THE CATS PROTECTION LEAGUE

To contact **The Cats Protection League,** write to:
The Cats Protection League
17 Kings Road
Horsham
West Sussex RH13 5PN

Tel: 01403 221900 (general enquiries)
        01403 221927 (Helpline)
Fax: 01403 218414
Web site: http://www.cats.org.uk

In addition, we have over 240 voluntary Branches and 13 Headquarters-run Shelters throughout the UK which between them rehome some 75,000 rescued cats every year.

JOIN THE CATS PROTECTION LEAGUE

You can support our work by becoming a member. We now have over 48,000 members whose modest subscription includes a free copy of our bi-monthly journal, *The Cat*, a publication which has been in circulation since 1934. This much loved and widely read journal has grown with the League and its articles, news, photographs, letters and Branch information show the caring attitude of Members and unpaid Branch volunteers nationwide. Junior members (13–18 years) receive *The Cat*, whilst Kitten Club members (under 13 years) receive three copies of *Junior News* alternating with three copies of *The Kitten* annually. Our younger members are encouraged to feel part of the Kitten Club and send in photographs and stories about their own cats. Write to us at the address (above) for further information.

WHY NOT ADOPT A RESCUED CAT?

Our Shelters and voluntary Branches have many thousands of needy cats in their care awaiting new homes. If you would like to adopt a Cats Protection League cat, here's what to do.

1 Contact our Helpline who will give you details of your nearest CPL Shelter or voluntary Branch.

2 Telephone the Shelter or Branch. Remember that our Branches are run entirely by unpaid volunteers, many of whom have full-time jobs. You may need to ring in the evening or at some other specified time. Shelters are run by paid staff, so you can contact them by telephone during the day.

3 Our representative will ask you a few simple questions and, if all is well, will arrange to come and see you at home. Note that a home visit is an integral part of the League's homing procedure, so please don't be alarmed or offended by this.

4 We endeavour to match a cat with his new owner and therefore, having discussed your circumstances, our representative will direct you to a Branch foster home or a Shelter for you to adopt your new cat.

5 You will be asked to sign a simple adoption form before taking your cat home with you.

6 All our adult cats are neutered prior to rehoming. If you are adopting a kitten you will need to sign to say you agree to have the kitten neutered at the appropriate age.

7 Before you leave the foster home or Shelter, please consider making a donation. We don't charge for our cats, but it costs a minimum of